The Packers-Bears riv_____ _____, __ ____,__ _____ ___ ___. passion from both sides is incredible. Jim Rice has done a nice job of reviewing each game in the rivalry. This book certainly brings back memories for me, both of games I covered and games I watched on TV growing up. It also provides historical reference for games and details I was not aware of.

                Dennis Krause
                Time Warner Cable SportsChannel
                Packers Radio Network

In 92 Years, Jim Rice chronicles the dates and details of football's greatest rivalry in his enjoyable, easy to read style. Written for both the diehard fan and the newbie, Rice delights readers and does his due diligence in researching his work."

                Tamara Leigh
                Host: Trend on You!
                Linked Local Network

92 Years!
Bears-Packers 1921-2013

Lyle —
Go Packers, beat
"DA Bears!"
Jim Rue

About the Author

Jim Rice is originally from Long Island, New York. He is a former school superintendent who studies and writes about now writes about football history. In his first book, *Giant Cheeseheads*, Rice looks at the close connections between the New York *Football Giants* and the Green Bay Packers. *Great Games of the Gridiron*, then revisited the 33 NFL Championship Games *before* the first Super Bowl. Rice's latest work is 92 Years! a game-by-game account of the NFL's oldest rivalry.

Other books by Jim Rice

Giant Cheeseheads!
The Giant-Packer rivalry and the former Giants who helped the Packers become champions.

Great Games of the Gridiron
NFL Championship Games 1933-1965

August 2014
Giant Cheesehead Books
www.giantcheeseheads.com

Copyright 2014 Jim Rice
All Rights Reserved

For Susie & Cedar!

92 Years!
Bears-Packers   1921-2013

Table of Contents

Introduction   1-2
Game of a Lifetime!   3-6

- 1920s   7-18

Rivalry Stars: Halas, Driscoll, Grange, Lambeau, Lewellen, Hubbard

- 1930s   19-36

Rivalry Stars: Nagurski, Hewitt, Musso, Hinkle, Hutson, Herber

- 1940s   37-56

Rivalry Stars: Luckman, Turner, Kavanaugh, Canadeo, Fritsch, Craig

- 1950s   57-75

Rivalry Stars: George, Casares, Atkins, Dillon, Howton, Rote

- 1960s   76-95

Rivalry Stars: Ditka, Butkus, Sayers, Lombardi, Starr, Nitschke

- 1970s   96-112

Rivalry Stars: Buffone, Douglas, Brockington, McCarren,

- 1980s   113-131

Rivalry Stars: McMahon, Payton, Singletary, Marcol, Dickey, Majkowski

- 1990s   132-151

Rivalry Stars: Harbaugh, Anderson, Butler Favre, White, Holmgren

- 2000s   152-169
Rivalry Stars: Urlacher, Hester, Briggs,
Favre, Driver, Woodson

- 2010s   170-178

- Appendix:
Wins, Championships, Coaches,   179-183
Payton, Favre, Stadiums

- Notes, Books, Internet   184-185

Introduction...

World War I had ended and the *Roaring Twenties* were off and running when the Bears first met the Packers in 1921. The Bears were called the Staleys then, and when George Halas purchased the club the following year, he changed their name to the Bears.

"Papa Bear" Halas believed that there was an appetite for pro football after the best players finished college. With that vision, he guided the new NFL and his Bears from infancy to stardom. His steady leadership guided the league past college football and pro baseball in popularity. To date, his Bears have won nine NFL championships, and many of his *Monsters of the Midway* are household names including Nagurski, Luckman, Ditka, Butkus, Sayers and Payton.

The Green Bay Packer franchise debuted in 1921 thanks to Curly Lambeau's employer, the Indian Packing Company. The company helped the team with jerseys, a practice field and, unexpectedly, a name – the Packers. With publicity generated by the hometown Press Gazette, many of their players and coaches became legendary: Hutson, Canadeo, Lombardi, Starr, Nitschke, Favre and White. The Packers are the only non-profit, community-owned franchise in professional sports and they have won 13 championships to date.

In the league' first 25 years, the Bears and Packers won nearly half of its championships (12). They have played one another twice a year since 1925* and, sometimes, they tangled three times. The week before each game, the intensity on both sides was unmistakable. Practices were more focused, and team rules more strictly adhered to. At times, the teams even installed completely new plays and formations just for this game!

"If either team ended up with a losing season, the year was considered a success if they had beaten Chicago or Green Bay."[1] That was the way Chicago quarterback Billy Wade put it, and fans would certainly agree. For that reason, here are all 188 *championship* games, as well as all the entertaining antics surrounding pro football's marquee rivalry.

* Not in 1982 due to the player's strike.

Game of a Lifetime!

12/29/13
Packers 33-28   Soldier Field   62,708

Of the 188 games between them, the most recent rivalry game was an instant classic, especially for Packer fans. Game 188 was so good that it leads off this book, and it already holds a special place in Green Bay Packer history.   Consider these facts.

- The Packers hadn't played the Bears on the final day of the regular season with a division title on the line since 1932!

- The winner would make the playoffs. No *wild card* berth for the loser.

- Packer quarterback Aaron Rodgers returned to the field for the first time since breaking his collarbone against the Bears on November 2, 2013.

- Green Bay receiver Randall Cobb also returned to the field for the first time after breaking his leg in October 20, 2013.

- In the fourth quarter, the Packers came from behind with two touchdowns. The winning score came on the *third* fourth down of Green Bay's the final drive.

- On fourth and eight, from the Chicago 48, Rodgers launched the winner with 43 seconds left. Thanks to John Kuhn's block, Rodgers escaped being sacked by Julius Peppers.

Green Bay won the NFC North and went on to the playoffs. The season had been a tough one for Green Bay as they limped to the end of the season with an injured quarterback and a broken defense. The downward spiral began on November 2, 2013 when Shea McClellan sacked Aaron Rodgers and broke his left collarbone. The Packers lost four of their next seven games, and their playoff hopes plummeted.

Without Rodgers, over the next seven games, the offense scored eight fewer points per game (- 8.57) while the defense gave up eight more (+ 8.14). This 16 point swing should have decimated Green Bay's season. But the combined record of Chicago and Detroit during Rodgers' absence (5-9) enabled Green Bay to go into the final game of the season trailing the Bears by only one-half game.

After weekly speculation about his return, Rodgers was back on the field for the final game against the Bears. In the first half, he threw without difficulty (15 of 22), and he drove the Packers into Bear territory before throwing two interceptions to kill both drives. The first pick was by safety Chis Conte (remember that name!) and the Bears capitalized with an 80 yard drive capped off by Matt Forte's first touchdown.

Late in the half, the Packers were at the Bears' 17 yard line. As Rodgers began to throw, the ball was knocked from his hand by Julius Peppers. The ball rolled on the ground, and the Bears assumed it was an incomplete pass. But the whistle had not blown. On his second try, Jared Boykin nonchalantly scooped up the ball. He was quickly urged by Rodgers and the Packers' bench to run it in. He did running untouched into the end zone!

In the third quarter, the Bears went back in front 14-13 when Matt Forte scored his second touchdown after Devin Hester's 49 yard punt return. The Packers then responded with an 84 yard drive in seven plays with Rodgers finding Randall Cobb for six. The Bears weren't fazed and in three plays they were back on top 21-20! Green Bay followed with a three and out, and Forte again led the Bears down the field to the Packer five yard line. On the first play of the fourth quarter, quarterback Jay Cutler found receiver Brandon Marshall for a touchdown. 28-20 Bears.

Rookie Eddie Lacy finished off the Packers' next drive with a 7 yard touchdown run around left end. It cut the lead to one (28-27) with 11:30 remaining. When Chicago couldn't move the ball on their next possession, Green Bay got it back on their 13 yard line with just over six minutes left.

To this point, Rodgers had completed 21 of his 31 passes. He would need a few more to beat the archrival Bears who had nearly derailed his season in November. Rodgers took charge of the moment and delivered. Starting at the 13, Rodgers moved the Packers steadily down the field. Three fourth downs later and with 46 seconds left to go, Rodgers dropped back to pass. With Julius Peppers bearing down on him, Rodgers threw a pass over the head of Chris Conte to Randall Cobb for the winning touchdown!

The Packers beat their archrivals on the road in the final seconds to win the NFC North. The loss knocked the Bears out of the playoffs. On Green Bay's last two drives, Aaron Rodgers completed 8 of 11 passes and ran for a key first down. His dramatic last minute connection with Cobb is already among the greatest plays in Packer history.

- The Bears now lead the series 93-89-6.

- The Packers have not led since 1932 when they enjoyed an 11-10-4 advantage.

- Chicago's current four game lead is their smallest advantage since 1941.

- The lead was first narrowed to four on 12/16/12. Last year's win brought it back to four.

Packers 0 13 7 13 33
Bears   7 0 14 7 28

Chi Forte 4yd pass from Cutler (Gould kick)
GB Crosby 33yd FG
GB Boykin 15yd fumble return (Crosby kick)
GB Crosby 27yd FG
Chi Forte 5yd run (Gould kick)
GB Cobb 7yd pass from Rodgers (Crosby kick)
Chi Forte 1 yd run (Gould kick)
Chi Marshall 5 yd pass from Cutler (Gould kick)
GB Lacy 6yd run (Crosby kick)
GB Cobb 48yd pass from Rodgers (two pt. conversion failed)

SEASON: Bears 8-8-0 (2nd)   Packers 8-7-1 (1st)

The Games
1921-29
Wins

Bears 7   3 Ties   Packers 6

Green Bay followed Chicago into the new National Football League in 1921. During the early years, the number of teams varied year-to-year. Twenty-two clubs competed in 1926, but just eight remained in 1932. The Great Depression had taken its toll.

At the beginning, pro football was a brutal, unpadded war that featured running plays on nearly every down. The forward pass was frowned upon and punting enjoyed a more prominent role in a team's offense. With a more oblong ball, punts traveled 70 to 80 yards. Teams could be pinned deep in their own territory against a defense that was ready to pounce on their first mistake.

Energetic supporters spread the excitement of the pro game in both Chicago and Green Bay. Legions of fans took trains to away games to support their team on the road. While Packer fans took to the rails in far greater numbers than Bear fans early on, the train rides were festive affairs for all the fans. Teams rode in private cars at the back of the train, and the *bar car* frequently became the center the entertainment. For the Bears, when they won, there were complimentary drinks and steaks for the players on the ride home. If they lost, the ride was far more somber.

The earliest games of the rivalry were hard fought, low scoring affairs. Players literally bludgeoned each other for a full 60 minutes as they played on both offense and defense. The Bears won seven of the first ten games (two ties), but the Packers learned quickly and took eight of the next ten (one tie). Both teams won their first championship in the twenties, and they quickly became two of the NFL's signature franchises.

1921

11/27
Chicago *Staleys* 20-0   Cubs Park   7,000

In the first game, the Staleys took a 14-0 first half lead over the Acme Packers before George Halas put the game completely out of reach with his fourth quarter touchdown catch. The Bears scored more points in this game against the Packers than any other team in the league. Green Bay's only scoring opportunities came on two unsuccessful field goal attempts by Curly Lambeau.

The first big hit of the rivalry – some would say cheap shot – came when John "Tarzan" Taylor of the Bears took a shot at big Howard "Cub" Buck (6' 3", 250lbs).

Packers 0 0 0 0   0
Staleys 0 14 0 6   20
Chi Stinchomb 45yd run (E. Sternaman kick)
Chi Pearce run (E. Sternaman kick)
Chi Halas pass from Harley (kick failed)

* More than 300 Packer fans and the Lumberjack Band took the train to Chicago. They arrived early and paraded through the Stratford Hotel and other downtown hotels and bars!

* After the season, Halas reported that the Packers had violated league rules by using college players in the game. In the spring of 1922, Green Bay was temporarily suspended from the league just long enough for Halas to sign one of the players who had played in the game for the Packers - Hunk Anderson of Notre Dame.

SEASON: Staleys 9-1-1 (1st)   Packers 3-2-1 (7th)
                NFL Champion

1922

No Game
After the game was scheduled, Halas demanded a $4,000 guarantee to bring the Bears to Green Bay on Thanksgiving Day. The Packers did not have the funds. The game was cancelled.

1923

10/14
Chicago *Bears* 3-0   **Bellevue Park**   **4,451**

This is the first of 124 consecutive games between the rivals. After taking over in 1921, Halas changed his team's name to the Bears, forging a not so subtle connection to the city's popular baseball team. In their first game against the Packers with their new name, a field goal by Ed "Dutch" Sternaman wins it for the Bears. Green Bay's two field goal attempts were unsuccessful.

At the time, this was the largest crowd to attend a sporting event in Northeastern Wisconsin.

Bears   0   3   0   0   3
Packers 0   0   0   0   0
Chi D. Sternaman 15yd FG

SEASON: Bears 9-2-1 (2nd)   Packers 7-2-1 (3rd)

1924

11/23
Bears 3-0   **Cubs Park**   **6,000**

The was a hotly contested game and, for the first time in NFL history, players were ejected for fighting – Frank Hanny of the Bears and Tillie Voss of Green Bay. The Bears won again thanks to a fumble by

Green Bay's Oscar Hendrian at the Packer 30 yard line. This time "Dutch" Sternaman's little brother, Joey, kicked the field goal.

Packers 0 0 0 0 0
Bears   0 0 3 0 3
Chi J. Sternaman 29yd FG

SEASON: Bears 6-1-4 (2nd)   Packers 7-4-0 (6th)

1925

9/27
Packers 14-10   City Stadium   5,389

To prepare for the Bears' first visit to new City Stadium, Curly Lambeau closed practices all week. It worked as Green Bay beat Chicago for the first time.

Both teams scored touchdowns on blocked punts. With the Bears in front by three in the fourth quarter, the Packers threatened. From the four yard line, Green Bay's Vern Lewellen fooled the Bears by throwing for a touchdown instead of running the ball.

* Thirty-two Bear-Packer games were played at City Stadium.

Bears   0 0 10 0 10
Packers 0 7 0 7 14
GB Gardner blocked punt recovery (Buck kick)
Chi J. Sternaman 30yd FG
Chi Murray blocked punt recovery (*Sternaman kick*)
GB Lewellen 4yd pass from Mathys (Buck kick)

11/22
Bears 21-0   **Cubs Park**   **6,398**

The Bears get revenge for their September loss in Green Bay. The Packers played without Curly Lambeau, and the Bears dominated play in front of their future teammate Harold "Red" Grange. Grange was on hand to watch the game after signing with the Bears earlier in the day. He would make his pro debut in Chicago's next game against their crosstown rival Cardinals.

Packers 0 0 0 0   0
Bears   0 7 0 14   21
Chi   Mohardt 3yd run (J. Sternaman kick)
Chi   J. Sternaman pass from Mohardt (J. Sternaman kick)
Chi   Knop pass from J. Sternaman (J. Sternaman kick)

SEASON: Bears 9-5-3 (7th)   Packers 8-5-0 (9th)

1926

9/26
Tie 6-6   **City Stadium**   **7,000**

This was an early NFL punting duel between Vern Lewellen of Green Bay and Paddy Driscoll of Chicago. With eight minutes left in the game and trailing 6-0, the Bears recovered a Packer fumble and tied it. But they failed to convert the extra point for the win. In the final minute, Curly Lambeau's long field goal attempt for Green Bay was unsuccessful.

Bears   0 0 0 6   6
Packers 0 0 6 0   6
GB   Lidberg 5yd run (kick failed)
Chi Driscoll 36yd pass from Walquist (kick failed)

11/21
Bears 19-13   **Cubs Park**   **7,000**

Paddy Driscoll of the Bears was the star in this edition of the rivalry game. He was involved in every Chicago scoring play and, in the fourth quarter, he returned a Packer fumble 40 yards for the winning touchdown! In a violent game, Frank Hanny of the Bears and Dick O'Donnell of the Packers were ejected for fighting.

Packers   6 7 0 0   13
Bears   6 3 3 7   19
GB   Lidberg 3yd run (kick failed)
Chi Hanny pass from Driscoll (kick failed)
Chi Driscoll 13yd FG
GB   Lewellen 40yd fumble recovery (Purdy kick)
Chi Driscoll 42yd FG
Chi Driscoll 40yd fumble recovery (Driscoll kick)

....

12/19
Tie 3-3   **Soldier Field**   **10,000**

The third game of 1926 was a fund raiser for *Paddy Carr's Christmas Basket Benefit.* It was played in freezing rain, but that didn't stop "Pid" Purdy of the Packers from nailing a 45 yard dropkick for a 3-0 lead. When Curly Lambeau fumbled a punt in the fourth quarter on his 15 yard line, Paddy Driscoll tied it for the Bears.

* This is the first game for the Packers at new Soldier Field.

Packers   0 0 3 0   3
Bears   0 0 0 3   3
GB   Purdy 45yd FG
Chi Driscoll 20yd FG

SEASON: Bears 12-1-3 (2nd)   Packers 7-3-3 (5th)

1927

10/2
Bears 7-6   City Stadium   5,500

The Packers scored late in the fourth quarter and left it up to Pid Purdy to tie the game with the extra point. Before the kick, Chicago's George Trafton shouted at Purdy about on the importance of the kick and the consequences of a miss. It worked!

After retiring, Hall of Famer George Trafton coached the Packers offensive line for one year.

Bears   0 7 0 0   7
Packers 0 0 0 6   6
Chi Senn TD run (Driscoll kick)
GB   Lewellen TD run (kick failed)

....

11/20
Bears 14-6   Wrigley Field   6,000

This game was won through the air and not on the ground. Both teams enjoyed success throwing the ball and Bears' halfback Bill Seen caught both touchdown passes for Chicago. His second one was an exciting 52 yard pass play to win it in the fourth quarter. Though Green Bay lost both games to the Bears in 1927, they finished ahead of Chicago in the standings for the first time as ties were not counted in a team's record until 1933.

Packers 0 0 6 0   6
Bears   0 7 0 7   14
Chi Senn 28yd pass from Driscoll (J. Sternaman kick)
GB   Enright 11yd pass from Dunn (Kick failed)
Chi Senn 52yd pass from Driscoll (Driscoll kick)

The Lumberjack Band again made the trip!

SEASON: Bears 9-3-2 (3rd)   Packers 7-2-1 (2nd)

1928

9/30
Tie 12-1   **City Stadium**   **10,000**

A record crowd witnessed an exciting 80 yard punt return that put Chicago up by two touchdowns at halftime. Singlehandedly, Vern Lewellen led the Green Bay comeback in the second half. With 15 seconds left and a chance to win it, Harry O'Boyle of the Packers missed a 25 yard field goal attempt.

Bears   6 6 0 0   12
Packers 0 0 6 6   12
Chi J. Sternaman 3yd run (kick failed)
Chi Sturtridge 80yd punt return (kick failed)
GB   Lewellen 15yd pass from Kotal (kick failed)
GB   Lewellen 2yd run (kick failed)

....

10/21
Packers 16-6   **Wrigley Field**   **15,000**

This is the Packers' first win in Chicago! Twenty-five hundred Green Bay fans traveled south to witness it. Bruce Jones' fourth quarter interception return clinched the victory for the Packers.

Packers 3 7 0 6   16
Bears   0 0 0 6   6
GB   O'Boyle 37yd FG
GB   Lewellen 1yd run (O'Boyle kick)
Chi Romney 1yd run (kick failed)
GB   Jones interception (kick failed)

12/9
Packers 6-0　　　　　**Wrigley Field**　　　　　**14,000**

This was the fifth straight road game for Green Bay. In a scoreless game with less than two minutes left, Green Bay quarterback Red Dunn faked a run and threw long to Dick O'Donnell to win the game. The win proved that Green Bay's win in October was no fluke. It also showed that the team from Wisconsin could compete against teams from the big cities!

Packers 0 0 0 6 6
Bears　 0 0 0 0 0
G B O'Donnell 60yd pass from Dunn (kick failed)

SEASON:　Bears 7-5-1 (5th)　　Packers 6-4-3 (4th)

1929

9/29
Packers 23-0　　　　　**City Stadium**　　　　　**13,000**

Fans packed City Stadium to watch Red Grange play for the Bears. Grange had returned to Chicago after one year with the New York Yankees of the rival American Football League. An overflow crowd eagerly hustled for spots along the fence that surrounded the field. The Packers were dominant in this early season matchup. They held the Bears to just five first downs, and Grange did very little.

Bears　 0 0 0 0　 0
Packers 0 14 9 0 23
GB McCrary run (Dunn kick)
GB Nash 15 yd pass from Blood (Dunn kick)
GB Safety
GB Molenda 10yd run (Dunn kick)

11/10
Packers 14-0   Wrigley Field   13,000

In a rainstorm, Hurdis McCrary scored both Packer touchdowns – one on offense and one on defense. Johnny Blood's great punting kept the Bears in their own territory, and the defense recorded its fourth shutout.

Big Cal Hubbard of the Packers was ejected for punching Bill Fleckenstein of the Bears.

Packers 0 0 14 0 14
Bears   0 0 0 0 0
GB McCrary pass from Dunn (Dunn kick)
GB McCrary pass interception (Dunn kick)

....

12/8
Packers 25-0   Wrigley Field   7,000

Red Grange picked up Chicago's only first down and the Packers won easily. Verne Lewellen and Eddie Kotal starred for Green Bay. Lewellen's punts averaged 60 yards.

This fourth straight shutout of the Bears, clinched Green Bay's first NFL championship! Twenty thousand fans welcomed the Packers home in downtown Green Bay at the Chicago Northwestern Train Depot. Many lined the railroad tracks to greet the team, and they lit flares to help guide the train home.

Packers 6 0 19 0 25
Bears   0 0 0 0 0
GB Lidberg run (kick failed)
GB Lewellen run (kick failed)
GB Kotal pass from Dunn (Dunn kick)
GB Kotal pass from Lewellen (kick failed)

SEASON: Bears 4-9-2 (9th)   Packers 12-0-1 (1st)

Rivalry Stars of the 1920s

George "Papa Bear" Halas   1921-1982   Coach & Owner

Halas is the father of pro football. He was the league's most formidable figure in its first 70 years and he coached the Bears to eight league championships. Halas brought pro football to the big cities. He believed the *forward pass* and *free substitution* (among many other initiatives) would make the game more exciting, and attract more talent. He was a visible supporter *for* the referendum that built City Stadium (now Lambeau Field). His coaching record was 324-151-31, and he referred to the rivalry as "the happiest series of games."[2]

John "Paddy" Driscoll   1926-29   QB

After seven years with the Chicago Cardinals, Driscoll was traded crosstown in 1926. In his four years as the Bears' quarterback, he was impressive. His 86 points in 1926 was a record until Don Hutson's 95 points in 1941. Driscoll was also a fine punter and drop-kicker. When Halas temporarily stepped aside in 1956 and 1957, he tapped Driscoll to coach his Bears.

Harold "Red" Grange   1929-34   HB, S

When the pro game played second fiddle to college football, *The Galloping Ghost* brought the new league credibility. He signed with the Bears right after a great collegiate career, and his exciting play generated national interest in pro football. In 1925, Grange drew 73,000 fans to the Polo Grounds, and he's credited with helping save the Giants' franchise. Grange left the Bears for two years before returning in 1929. He was first team All-Pro in 1930 and 1931.

Earl "Curly" Lambeau   1921-194   Coach, RB/QB

Who would have imagined that Curly Lambeau's tonsillitis would lead to the founding of the Green Bay Packers? When Lambeau did not return to Notre Dame due to the illness, he began the process that would lead Green Bay into the NFL in 1921. When Lambeau played, he was the first Packer to pass for more than 1,000 yards in season. In his tenure as coach, Lambeau was a strong advocate of the forward pass and, like Halas, his contributions go far beyond his own team. His 29 year coaching record in Green Bay was 212-106-21.

Vern Lewellen   1924-32   HB, P, QB

Lewellen was a great versatile player who could run, pass and punt with the best players of his day. From 1926-29, he was a first team All-Pro running back, and he scored 51 touchdowns for Green Bay. While records are scarce from the twenties, Lewellen's punts were legendary. With a more rounded ball, some of them went 80 yards! Twenty years after retiring, he was the Packers' General Manager from 1954-58.

Cal "The Enforcer" Hubbard   1929-33, 1935   T, DT

Hubbard graduated from Geneva College. After playing on the 1927 champion New York Giants, Hubbard requested a trade to Green Bay. At 6' 2" and 250 pounds, he was one of the biggest and most-feared players of his day. He was so powerful that he could easily toss aside most players. Occasionally, Lambeau would drop Hubbard off the line of scrimmage, like a linebacker, to disrupt receivers and ball carriers. Hubbard helped lead Green Bay to three straight titles in 1929-31.

The Games
1930-39
Wins
Bears 12   1 Tie   Packers 11
Series: 19-17-4 Bears

The Great Depression hit the NFL hard with five franchises declaring bankruptcy. The ten teams that remained in 1933 were divided into two divisions, in part, to avoid a repeat of the 1932 championship controversy. The division winners would meet in a winner-take-all championship game. The excitement of a final game to end each season appealed to the owners and to George Halas.

In the thirties, rule changes supported by Halas helped to increase passing and scoring which made the game more exciting. Passes could now be thrown from *anywhere* behind the line of scrimmage instead of the previously required five yards back. Playbooks exploded with new plays and formations and the ball was also slimmed down to make it more aerodynamic. Hash marks brought the game toward the center of the field to give offenses more options.

Passing and speed made the game more exciting. New stars like speedy Don Hutson and the strong-armed Sammy Baugh gave pro football the boost it needed to distinguish itself from the college game. More fans saw the action too when *moving pictures* brought weekly NFL highlights to movie theatres around the country. Millions of new fans began following pro football and the NFL Draft formally began in 1936.

When the Bears came north to play Green Bay, they stayed at the Northland Hotel. After a noisy night's sleep, they dressed in the hotel and took buses to City Stadium, jeered all the way. The rivalry game began to attract interest from national audiences when the Bears and the Packers won six of the league's first 14 championships. The rivalry games were typically close and hard fought. As rule changes encouraged more passing, the run only, smash mouth style of football came to an end. The forward pass began its long climb from near obscurity to the most dominant element of the game today.

1930

9/28
Packers 7-0   **City Stadium**   **13,000**

As the NFL defending champion, the Packers opened with consecutive shutouts of the Cardinals and the Bears. The shutout of the Bears was their fifth straight over their border rival. This game was Bronco Nagurski's (6' 2", 235lbs) first against the Packers. Green Bay held Nagurski and the great Red Grange to just 48 yards. An interception by "Bo" Molenda led to the game's only points.

In 1930-32, Halas stepped aside from coaching and named Ralph Jones of Lake Forest College (and Illinois) to succeed him.

Bears   0   0   0   0
Packers   0   7   0   0   7
GB   Lewellen 1yd run (Dunn kick)

....

11/9
Packers 13-12   **Wrigley Field**   **25,000**

Bronco Nagurski kept Chicago in the game, but two missed extra points by Walt Homer sunk the Bears. Nagurski gained 104 of Chicago's 196 total yards! During the game, Cal "The Enforcer" Hubbard wanted "a shot" at the rookie Nagurski. Red Grange agreed to step aside to let the two go at it! Hubbard learned quickly that he wanted nothing further to do with Mr. Nagurski.

* Three thousand Packer fans attended. For those did not go, they listened to the game on the first radio broadcast of a Packer game from Chicago. Thousands of fans also welcomed the team home.

Packers 0 6 0 7   13
Bears   0 0 6 6   12
GB Blood 17yd pass from Lewellen (kick failed)
Chi J.Sternaman 33yd run (kick failed)
GB Lewellen 19yd pass from Dunn (Dunn kick)
Chi Brumbaugh 1yd run (kick failed)

....

12/7
Bears 21-0 **Wrigley Field** **20,000**

Six interceptions spelled doom for Green Bay's seven game winning streak against the Bears. "Red" Grange had two of them, both of which led to touchdowns. The favored Packers were run over by Grange and Bronco Nagurski. The Bears' strong running attack opened the way for the passing game and Luke Johnsos' two touchdown passes.

Packers 0 0 0 0   0
Bears   0 7 0 14 21
Chi Johnsos 21yd pass from Brumbaugh (Johnsos kick)
Chi Johnsos 30yd pass from Brumbaugh (Johnsos kick)
Chi Nesbitt 38yd run (Grange pass)

SEASON: Bears 9-4-1 (3rd)   Packers 10-3-1 (1st)

1931

9/27
Packers 7-0 **City Stadium** **15,000**

A hot day brought out a record number of Packer fans to see the hometown team take on Bronco Nagurski and Red Grange. The Packer defense stopped them both, and the Bears got inside the Packers'

20 yard line only once. A fumble by Chicago halfback Joe Lintzenich led to Green Bay's only points.

Bears   0 0 0 0   0
Packers   0 0 7 0   7
GB Lewellen 2yd run

....

11/1
Packers 6-2   **Wrigley Field**   **30,000**

In another brutal contest, Cal Hubbard deflected a pass that was intercepted by Mike Michalske and returned 80 yards for the game's only touchdown! Chicago often threatened, but they came away empty handed after being inside the Packer 25 yard line six times. The win put the Packers in first place.

Packers   0 6 0 0   6
Bears   0 0 2 0   2
GB Michalske 80yd interception return (kick failed)
Chi Safety, Johnsos tackled Dunn in end zone

....

12/6/
Bears 7-6   **Wrigley Field**   **18,000**

Joe Lintzenich made-up for his September fumble and Chicago backed-up his early touchdown with great defense. Green Bay's only points came when Johnny "Blood" McNally caught a touchdown pass when Red Grange fell down in the end zone. Unfortunately, the usually reliable Red Dunn missed the extra point.

Chicago's defense stopped the Green Bay offense that scored 116 more points than their opponents in 1931.

Packers   0 6 0 0   6
Bears   7 0 0 0   7
Chi Lintzenich 28yd pass from Brumbaugh (Tackwell kick)
GB Blood 28 yard pass from Lewellen (kick failed)

SEASON: Bears 8-5-0 (3rd)   Packers 12-2-0 (1st)

1932

9/25
Tie 0-0   **City Stadium**   **13,000**

This was a tough, defensive battle with 26 punts and just 13 first downs. It was also the first meeting of Green Bay's rookie Clarke Hinkle and the Bronco Nagurski. Their first collision caused a seven inch cut to be opened under Hinkle's chin. Near the end of the game, a field goal attempt by Chicago never got off the ground thanks to a bad snap.

During one of Green Bay's kickoffs, Chicago's George Trafton ran up and kicked the ball causing a near riot with Lambeau and Halas arguing with each other on the field!

Bears   0 0 0 0
Packers 0 0 0 0
     --- ---

....

10/16
Packers 2-0   **Wrigley Field**   **17,500**

In the second quarter, Tom Nash of the Packers blocked Dick Nesbitt's punt out of the end zone for the winning safety! Chicago threatened behind Nagurski's 86 yards rushing, but could never score.

Before this game, the Bears had played three games that all ended 0-0.

Packers 0 2 0 2
Bears   0 0 0 0
GB Blocked punt / safety by Nash

12/11
Bears 9-0   **Wrigley Field**   **5,000**

In the game that derailed the Packers' hopes for a fourth consecutive championship, four inches of snow and brisk winds pounded Wrigley for the decisive matchup. Thousands of fans stayed home rather than brave the weather!

Chicago broke a scoreless tie in the fourth quarter. After the field goal, Nagurski's long romp put the game out of reach. The Bears' victory stopped the Packers' drive for a fourth title in a row. It also began a vigorous debate over which team deserved the 1932 NFL title ... the 6-1-6 Bears? the 6-1-4 Spartans? or the 10-3-1 Packers?

In 1932, ties were not counted in a team's record. Consequently, both the Bears and the Spartans (the future Detroit Lions) finished with a higher winning percentage than the Packers. Chicago then beat the Spartans in a playoff game and won the 1932 title with a 7-1-6 record.

* Due to the low turnout for this game, Halas added insult to injury when he paid only $1,000 of the $2,500 game guarantee. He gave the Packers an I.O.U. for the balance!

Packers   0 0 0 0   0
Bears   0 0 0 9   9
Chi Engebretsen 14yd FG
Chi Nagurski 54yd touchdown run (kick failed)

SEASON: Bears 7-1-6 (1st)   Packers 10-3-1 (2nd)
                NFL Champion

1933

9/24
Bears 14-7　　　　　　**City Stadium**　　　　　　12,000

The Packers led 7-0 until the last five minutes when Bill Hewitt of the Bears took over the game. After marching the Bears to midfield in just three plays, Hewitt connected with Luke Johnsos on an end-around-option play for a long touchdown. Chicago stopped Green Bay on their next possession when Hewitt blasted through the left side of the Packer line and blocked Arnie Herber's punt. Hewitt then picked up the bouncing football and scored the winning touchdown!

In the second quarter, on a faked punt, Hinkle knocked Nagurski out of the game with a vicious hit to the face along the sidelines. The collision was described as a "sickening thud."[3]

* The sudden turnaround in the fourth quarter had some fans wondering if the game was fixed!

* Red Grange wanted the game ball, but the Packers' ballboy would not give it to him.

```
Bears    0  0  0  14  14
Packers  0  0  7  0   7
```
GB Goldenberg 1yd run Monnett kick)
Chi Johnsos 46yd pass from Bill Hewitt (Manders kick)
Chi Hewitt recovered blocked punt in end zone (Manders kick)

....

10/22
Bears 10-7　　　　　　**Wrigley Field**　　　　　　19,000

This battle was very similar to the previous battle. This time, Chicago scored 10 points in the final *four* minutes. The winning points came after a partially blocked punt gave the ball to the Bears at their 43 yard line. A few plays later, "Automotic" Jack Manders kicked the winner.

* The defeat ended Green Bay's hopes of playing in the first NFL Championship Game scheduled at the end of the season.

Packers 0 7 0 0 7
Bears 0 0 0 10 10
GB Blood 43yd pass from Herber (Monnett kick)
Chi Johnsos 24yd pass from Red Grange (Manders kick)
Chi Manders 30yd FG

....

12/10
Bears 7-6   **Wrigley Field**   **7,000**

The Bears swept the season series when Gene Ronzani (future coach of the Packers) scored Chicago's touchdown. Green Bay's fourth quarter touchdown went for naught when the extra point attempt was blocked by former Packer, Joe Zeller! The Packers finish the season with a losing record for the first time.

* Green Bay quarterback Arnie Herber didn't play because of a car accident three days before the game.

Packers 0 0 0 6 6
Bears 0 7 0 0 7
Chi Ronzani 42yd pass from Molesworth (Manders kick)
GB Monnett 85yd punt return (kick blocked)

SEASON: Bears 10-2-1 (1st)   Packers 5-7-1 (3rd)
                Beat Giants 23-21 in
                first title game

1934

9/23
Bears 24-10   **City Stadium**   **14,000**

Another strong finish by Chicago ran their winning streak over the Packers to five. The Bears snapped a 10-10 tie in the fourth quarter when Bronco Nagurski scored two touchdowns. One of his touchdown runs was a long rumble down the sidelines to cap off a great afternoon of 93 yards rushing.

```
Bears    3  0  7  14   24
Packers  0  3  7   0   10
```
Chi Manders 24yd FG
GB   Monnett 16yd FG
Chi Hewitt 7yd pass from Nagurski (Manders kick)
GB   Goldenberg 11yd run (Monnett kick)
Chi Nagurski 1yd run (Manders kick)
Chi Nagurski 40yd run (Manders kick)

....

10/28
Bears 27-14   Wrigley Field   11,000

Chicago's running game was the league's best in 1934. Bronco Nagurski, Gene Ronzani and Beattie Feathers ran for over 2,000 yards. In this game, Feathers opened and closed the contest with touchdowns. The speedy back from Tennessee followed Bronco Nagurski through Green Bay's defense for 155 yards. As a team, the Bears ran for 339 yards!

```
Packers  0  7  0   7   14
Bears    7  3  7  10   27
```
Chi Feathers 18yd pass from Ronzani (Manders kick)
GB   Rose 9yd pass from Monnett (Monnett kick)
Chi Manders 18yd FG
Chi Brumbaugh 27yd pass from Ronzani (Manders kick)
Chi Manders 28yd FG
GB   Dilweg 13yd pass from Herber (Hinkle kick)
Chi Feathers 46yd run (Nagurski kick)

SEASON: Bears 13-0-0 (1st)   Packers 7-6-0 (3rd)
          Lost to Giants 30-13
             in title game

1935

9/22
Packers 7-0   **City Stadium**   **13,600**

The first play from scrimmage changed pro football forever! The remarkable touchdown pass that Arnie Herber uncorked from his 17 yard line stunned the packed stadium. Herber, connected with rookie Don Hutson at midfield for a spectacular 83 yard touchdown play. The ball traveled 66 yards in the air and Hutson never broke stride as he blew past Beattie Feathers of Chicago for the touchdown.

The first Herber to Hutson touchdown bomb provided all of the scoring. It ended Chicago's six game winning streak over Green Bay and, more importantly, it changed the NFL forever.

Bears   0 0 0 0
Packers 7 0 0 7
GB Huston 83yd pass from Herber (Monnett kick)

....

10/27
Packers 17-14   **Wrigley Field**   **29,386**

Don Hutson does it again. Green Bay's amazing comeback was so unlikely that many Packer fans had already left for Wiscosnin on the *milk train.*

With two and one-half minutes remaining, the Packers trailed 14-3. Arnie Herber struck wtwo quick touchdowns to Don Hutson. With the Bears staying back to prevent a long pass, Herber found Hutson in the flat and he sprinted his way past the Chicago defense for a 65 yard touchdown! Chicago quarterback Bernie Masterson then fumbled on the Bears' next possession. Green Bay tackle Ernie Smith recovered the ball on the Chicago 13 yard line. With 10 seconds left, Herber found Hutson again to win it, and Packer fans who left early couldn't believe the news when they got back to Wisconsin.

Packers   0   3   0   14   17
Bears   0   0   7   7   14
GB   Schwammel 18yd FG
Chi Ronzani 44yd pass from Masterson (Manders kick)
Chi Sisk 55yd run
GB   Hutson 65yd pass from Herber (Schwammel kick)
GB   Hutson 4yd pass from Herber (Smith kick)

Season: Bears 6-4-2 (3rd)   Packers 8-4-0 (2nd)

1936

9/20
Bears 30-3   **City Stadium**   **14,312**

The Bears smack down the Packers and hand them their in only loss of the season. They held Green Bay to just three points in one of their worst defeats at home.

The first half was relatively close. A double lateral put Chicago in front to stay, and four different players eventually scored for the Bears. Early in the third quarter, they took complete control of the game with a short touchdown toss to the great "Stinky" Hewitt.

Emmet Platten, a Green Bay radio personality, protested a call by running on the field. He punched a Chicago player before being restrained.

Bears   3   7   6   14   30
Packers   0   3   0   0   3
Chi Manders 36yd FG
GB   Schwammel 26yd FG
Chi Ronzani 12yd lateral from Johnsos, lateral from Hewitt, pass from Molesworth (Manders kick)
Chi Hewitt 12yd pass from Ray Nolting (kick failed)
Chi Brumbaugh 5yd pass from Molesworth (Manders kick)
Chi Karr 9yd run (Manders kick)

11/1
Packers 21-10   **Wrigley Field**   **31,346**

This time around, the Packers hand the Bears their first loss of the season. After a quick start by Chicago, the game belonged to Green Bay.

Herber to Hutson struck again in the second quarter. Clarke Hinkle then put Green Bay in front with a remarkable 59 yard run touchdown run. On this run, Hinkel was hit so hard by Bronco Nagurski that he flew backwards past Chicago's George Musso who had already missed tackling him. Hinkle landed on his feet and kept running for an amazing touchdown. After the victory, the Packers and Bears were tied for first in the Western Divison at 6-1.

* This was the biggest Bears' crowd since Red Grange's debut in 1925!

Packers 0 14 0 7   21
Bears   10   0 0 0   10
Chi Manders 23yd FG
Chi Hewitt 53yd fumble return (Manders kick)
GB Hutson 9yd pass from Herber (Smith kick)
GB Hinkle 59yd run (Smith kick)
GB Sauer 2yd run (Engebretsen kick)

SEASON: Bears 9-3-0 (2nd)   Packers 10-1-1 (1st)
         Beat Boston Redskins
         21-6 in title game

1937

9/19
Bears 14-2   **City Stadium**   **16,658**

With Green Bay quarterback Arnie Herber out of action due to a shoulder injury, points would be hard to come by for Green Bay. A scoreless first half for both teams finally gave way to a third quarter that had all the action. The Bears scored two quick touchdowns with Ray Notlting and Jack Manders providing the offensive fireworks. Green Bay's only points came when Don Hutson blocked a Sam Francis punt out of the end zone for a safety. The Bears intercepted four Green Bay passes in the fourth quarter to close out the win.

Bears   0 0 14 0 14
Packers 0 0   2 0   2
Chi Nolting 2yd run (Manders kick)
Chi Manders 45yd pass from Masterson (Manders kick)
GB   Safety, Hutson recovered blocked punt in end zone

....

11/7
Packers 24-14   Wrigley Field   44,977

The Packers knock the Bears from the ranks of the undefeated again. Chicago never recovered from an explosive second quarter by the Packers. The 17 point assault began with Arnie Herber's spectacular 76 yard touchdown pass to Don Hutson. In the third quarter, two long touchdowns brought the Bears back to within three. Herber, Hutson and Clarke Hinkle then drove the Packers downfield in the fourth quarter for the decisive points.

Packers 0 17 0   7 24
Bears   0   0 14 0 14
GB   Hutson 76yd pass from Herber (Hinkle kick)
GB   Smith 21yd FG
GB   Jankowski 23yd interception return (Smith kick)
Chi Manders 55yd interception return (Manders kick)
Chi Manske 64yd pass from Masterson (Manders kick)
GB   Hinkle 4yd pass from Monnett (Engebretsen kick)

SEASON: Bears 9-1-1 (1st)   Packers 7-4-0 (2nd)
*Lost title game to
Redskins 28-21*

1938

9/18
Bears 2-0 **City Stadium** **15,172**

In a rainstorm, the field was a mud pit, and neither team came close to scoring. Finally, in the fourth quarter, a bad snap from center Darrell Lester of the Packers went over the head of punter Arnie Herber and into the end zone for a safety. With less than a minute remaining, Clarke Hinkle's 37 yard field goal attempt went wide right.

Bears   0 0 0 2   2
Packers 0 0 0 0   0
Chi Safety, Jones recovered fumble in end zone

....

11/6
Packers 24-17 **Wrigley Field** **40,208**

In the first few minutes of this very physical game, two costly fumbles by fullback Bert Johnson of the Bears allowed Green Bay to jump in front. They held on tight with several defensive stops in the second half. John Howell of the Packers blocked a pass on Chicago's final play to clinch the win and a split in the season series with Chicago.

* To motivate his players prior to the game, Curly Lambeau read them telegrams from fans that had been sent to the hotel.

* Bears' end Dick Plasman (the last player not to wear a helmet) crashed head first into the brick wall at Wrigley Field. It "peeled his head open..."[4] said Green Bay cornerback Herm Schneidman.

Packers 14 7 3 0   24
Bears   10 7 0 0   17
GB Hinkle 15yd pass from Monnett (Monnett kick)
GB Hutson 20 yd pass from Monnett (Monnett kick)
Chi Manders 7yd run (Manders kick)
Chi Manders 34yd FG
GB Jankowski 1yd run (Hutson kick)

Chi Karr 8yd pass from Swisher (Manders kick)
GB Hinkle 35 yd FG

SEASON: Bears 6-5-0(3rd)   Packers 8-3-0 (1st)
*Lost to Giants 23-17
in title game*

1939

9/24
Packers 21-16   **City Stadium**   **19,192**

Another brutal game with lots of action after the whistle. There were frequent fights and "altercations with officials and on nearly every play."5   In the first half, George Musso of the Bears and Russ Letlow of the Packers were ejected for fighting .

The Bears were in front 13-0 at halftime.   A long third quarter drive finally got the Packers on the scoreboard. They also recovered two Chicago fumbles that led to touchdowns. The three scores took control of the game for Green Bay and the defense then did its job by holding the Bears to three points in the second half.

* Prior to the game, Halas accused Packer fans of spying on practices with binoculars. Fans told him they were birdwatching!

Bears   0   13   0   3   16
Packers 0   0 21   0   21
Chi Osmanski 16yd run (Manders kick)
Chi Masterson 7yd run (kick failed)
GB Isbell 11yd run (Engebretsen kick)
GB Hinkle 1yd run (Engebretsen kick)
GB Greenfield, fumble recovery for touchdown (Engebretsen kick)
Chi Manders 35yd FG

11/5
Bears 30-27   **Wrigley Field**   **40,537**

A great battle with six lead changes! The Bears persevered and came from behind four times to claim victory. Chicago's three rookies put on quite a performance: quarterback Sid Luckman, fullback Bill Osmanski and halfback Bob MacLeod.

In the second quarter, Luckman and Osmanski connected for six to put the Bears in front 14-13. Green Bay grabbed the lead before halftime, and Chicago's veteran signal caller Bernie Masterson took it back for the Bears (23-20). Herber then found Hutson midway through the final quarter, and the Packers appeared to have put the game away 27-23.

But the Bears' rookies were not finished. Sid Luckman uncorked a long pass to Bob MacLeod that put Chicaho on the Green Bay 10 yard line. Osmanski then picked up the rest around left end, and the comeback was complete.

* There were numerous fist fights in this game. The fans even got into it. One of them had a rather unsuccessful encounter with former Packer Lavvie Dilweg.

* At a practice before the game, Lambeau saw men in white coats watching with binoculars. Halas claimed they were biologists!

Packers 13 7 0 7 27
Bears 7 10 6 7 30
GB Laws 72yd punt return (Smith kick)
Chi Swisher 57 yd run (Jack Manders kick)
GB Gantenbein 32yd pass from Isbell (kick failed)
Chi Osmanski 19yd pass from Luckman (Manders kick)
Chi Snyder 27yd FG
GB Jankowski 29yd pass from Isbell (Engebretsen kick)
Chi Plasman 8yd pass from Masterson (kick failed)
GB Hutson 20yd pass from Herber (Engebretsen kick)
Chi Osmanski 3yd run (Manders kick)

SEASON: Bears 8-3-0 (2nd)   Packers 9-2-0 (1st)
*Beat Giants 27-0
in title game*

Rivalry Stars of the 1930s

Bronco Nagurski   1930-37, 1943   FB/LB

Nagurski was an All-American at Minnesota. He was pure muscle and an outstanding player. He was the most intimidating player of his time. He ran over opponents rather than around them, averaging 4.4 yards per carry. He threw over them as well, and his passing won the NFL title for the Bears in 1932 and 1933. Defensively, Nagurski was so strong and fast, you couldn't escape him. In 1943, he came out of retirement at age 35 to help the Bears win the 1943 championship!

Bill "Stinky" Hewitt   1932-36   E/DE

After playing at Michigan, Hewitt joined the Bears for five seasons. He did not wear a helmet until he was required him to do so in 1939. Each year, Hewitt finished near the top of the league in catches and touchdowns. As a defensive end, Hewitt was tough to move, and he was called *The Offside Kid* because of his quick first step. In 1933, Hewitt's lateral helped the Bears win the first NFL Championship Game. His # 56 was one of the first to be retired by George Halas.

George Musso   1933-44   DT/OT

A four sport star at Millikin College, Musso played for the Bears for twelve years. Early in his career, Red Grange persuaded Musso to stay with Chicago and turndown an offer from the Packers. At 6' 2" and 270 pounds, Musso anchored the Bears line without wearing a helmet. On offense, he led the way for Bronco Nagurski and defensively, he handled the middle of the line. Musso was a team captain for nine years, and he played in seven championship games.

★

Arnie "Flash" Herber   1930-40   QB

A Green Bay native, Herber was the game's first great *long* passer. The strong armed Herber was a perfect fit for Curly Lambeau's passing offense. Herber played for the Packers from 1930-40, and he led the league in passing three times. He won two NFL championships and his passes to Don Hutson were spectacular. Herber-to-Hutson was the first great passing combination in pro football history.

Clarke Hinkle   1932-41   FB, LB

After graduating from Bucknell in 1932, Hinkle became one of the greatest two way players in Packer history. He could do everything: run, pass, catch, kick, punt, and tackle. In his 10-year career, he led Green Bay in rushing six times and he was the NFL's all-time leading rusher in 1941 when he retired (3,850 yards). As a very physical linebacker, Hinkle was a punishing tackler and his battles with Nagurski were legendary, especially their confrontation on 9/24/1933.

Don Hutson   1935-45   E, DE, DB

Hutson is one of the greatest receivers of all-time. From Alabama, his speed and athleticism were unmatched. His spectacular plays helped change pro football from a running game to a passing game. In 11 seasons, he led the NFL in catches eight times, touchdowns nine times and he played in four championship games (winning two). In the days before free substitution, Hutson was also a fine defender who intercepted 30 passes in his career. Hutson still holds six NFL records and 20 Green Bay records.

The Games
1940-49
Wins
Bears 16   1 Tie   Packers 4
Series: 35-21-5 Bears

More than 600 NFL players and coaches served during World War II. Twenty-two were killed in action. George Halas served for the second time from 1942-46, working alongside Admiral Nimitz. Though the quality of play slipped during the war, many former players came out of retirement to reinforce rosters and boost ticket sales.

In 1945, after winning the NFL championship, the Cleveland Rams decided to move to Los Angeles. In 1946, the All-American Football Conference (AAFC) began competing with the NFL. The color barrier was lifted in 1946, and the competition for players had never more keen. Other important developments in the game included: helmets became mandatory in 1943, and hash marks were moved five yards further from the sidelines to giving offenses more room to operate

The forties were especially good to the Bears who won four championships - 1940, 1941, 1943 and 1946. They crushed nearly everyone in their path. In the 1940 title game, they battered the Redskins 73-0 for the most-lopsided win in NFL history. *The Monsters of the Midway* were so deep on both sides of the ball that they dominated the league in 1941 and 1942 as well. They enjoyed an undefeated regular season in 1942 before stumbling in the title game to the revenge-seeking Redskins! Sid Luckman led the innovative T-formation offense, and their defense was outstanding.

The Packers finished second to the Bears every year from 1940-43. After World War II and through the early 1950s, the rivalry turned more violent. Sometimes, the games became more like wrestling matches. The Packers finally overcame the Bears in 1944 and went on to win the another championship. But for the remainder of the decade, Green Bay never finished higher than third. After 1946, the Bears continued to win, but they would not win claim another championship until 1963.

1940

9/22
Bears 41-10　　　　　　**City Stadium**　　　　　　**23,557**

In the first game of the season for the Bears, they showed how dominant they would soon become. They smothered the defending champion Packers at home forcing nine turnovers. Seven were interceptions, and two led to Chicago touchdowns.

The day's highlight was the two 90 yard punt returns. George McAfee struck first for 93 yards, and Ray Nolting's 97 yarder in the third quarter put the game away. McAfee also threw for a touchdown and ran for another as the Bears romped!

Since Chicago's season started one week later than Green Bay's, Halas and his staff scouted Green Bay in their opener against the Eagles.

Bears　7　7　14　13　41
Packers　3　0　7　0　10
GB　Engebretsen 25yd FG
Chi　McAfee 93yd kickoff return (Plasman kick)
Chi　Osmanski 1yd run (Manders kick)
Chi　Nolting 97yd kickoff return (Snyder kick)
GB　Hutson 35yd pass from Herber (Hutson kick)
Chi　Kavanaugh 8yd pass from McAfee (Artoe kick)
Chi　McAfee 9yd run (kick blocked)
Chi　Kavanaugh 39yd pass from Snyder (Manders kick)

11/3
Bears 14-7   **Wrigley Field**   **45,434**

The largest crowd in Chicago Bears' history witnessed a closely fought contest that featured all of the scoring in the first half. Chicago scored first, and the Packers tied it in the second quarter after they picked off Sid Luckman. Chicago came right back with Scooter McClean's 55 yard kickoff return which setup their second touchdown. In the second half, the Packers were inside the Bears' 35 yard line five times, but they came away empty handed.

Packers 0 7 0 7
Bears   7 7 0 14
Chi Maniaci 3yd run (Manders kick)
GB   Hutson 5yd pass from Herber (Engebretsen kick)
Chi Famiglietti 7yd run (Manders kick)

Season: Bears 8-3-0 (1st)   Packers 6-4-1 (2nd)
*Beat Redskins 73-0
for the title*

1941

9/28
Bears 25-17   **City Stadium**   **24,876**

Three Packer fumbles helped the Bears to open up a 15-0 lead before Green Bay's offense got going. Packer quarterback Cecil Isbell connected with Don Hutson for six, and then Clarke Hinkle did his share with a field goal and a touchdown. By the third quarter, the Packers had dug out their early hole and led 17-15. Chicago then took the lead away when George McAfee returned the kickoff 51 yards and then, a short time later, he scored from 13 yards out. A final field goal then iced the game for the Bears.

In his first rivalry game, some of Tony Canadeo's teeth were knocked out by the Bears' defensive line.

After this loss and in preparation for the rematch, Curly Lambeau gave guard Russ Letlow permission to travel to Chicago to scout Bears' home games.

Bears   6 9 7 3 25
Packers 0 10 7 0 17
Chi   Kavanaugh 63yd pass from McAfee (kick blocked)
Chi   Snyder 25yd FG
Chi   McLean 13yd run (kick failed)
GB   Hutson 45yd pass from Isbell (Hutson kick)
GB   Hinkle 40yd FG
GB   Hinkle 1 yd run (Hutson kick)
Chi   McAfee 13yd run (Stydahar kick)
Chi   Snyder 34yd FG

....

11/2
Packers 16-14   Wrigley Field   46,484

Four special trains carried more than 2,500 fans to Wrigley to see the Packers take on the undefeated Bears. What they saw was totally shocking! Green Bay handed the defending champions their only loss of the season. They did it with a seven man defensive line that held the Bears to just 65 yards rushing and 183 yards overall.

The Packers scored the first time they had the ball. In the first half, their defense held the Bears to just 25 yards. Falling behind 16-0, Chicago's offense finally woke up in the fourth quarter. They had cut the lead to nine with six minutes left, when George MacAfee's interception put the Bears at the Packer 15. Ray Nolting then took it in to cut the Packer lead to two. With three minutes left, Chicago got the ball back. When Halas decided not to attempt a field goal from the Packer 36, Luckman dropped back to pass and was sacked by Harry Jacunski to end the comeback.

* At the time, this was the largest crowd ever to watch a pro football game in the Midwest.

* Nine fans suffered heart attacks during the game including Halas' sister-in-law who died.

* Halas thought the '41 Bears was the best team he ever coached.

* Some Chicago fans thought the game was fixed. The Bears would not lose again until the 1942 championship game.

Packers 6 0 10 0 16
Bears   0 0   0 14 14
GB Isbell 2yd run (kick blocked)
GB Brock 36yd pass from Isbell (Hutson kick)
GB Hinkle 43 yard FG
Chi Standlee 8yd run (Snyder kick)
Chi Nolting 1yd run (Stydahar kick)

SEASON: Bears 10-1-0 (1st)   Packers 10-1-0 (1st)

1941 Western Division Playoff Game

12/14
Bears 33-14   **Wrigley Field**   **43,425**

The rivalry game makes an appearance in the postseason. One week after Pearl Harbor, the Bears and Packers met for the third time in 1941 as they both finished the regular season tied atop the Western Division at 10-1-1. Prior to 2010, this was the only postseason game between the rivals.

With temperatures in the teens, Chicago's Hugh Gallarneau fumbled the opening kickoff, and the Packers jumped in front 7-0. When they did not capitalize on a second Chicago turnover in the first quarter, the Bears collected themselves and ran off 30 unanswered points. This time around, the Bears were ready for Green Bay's seven man front, and they rolled over the Packers with 267 yards rushing. Green Bay ran for a paltry 33 yards. Norm Standlee had the greatest game of his career, and the powerful *Monsters of the Midway* would go on to win their second consecutive NFL title.

```
Packers   7   0   7   0   14
Bears     6  24   0   3   33
```
GB   Hinkle 1yd run (Hutson kick)
Chi   Standlee 3yd run (Stydahar kick)
Chi   Standlee 2yd run (Stydahar kick)
Chi   Swisher 9yd run (Stydahar kick)
GB   Van Every 10yd pass from Isbell (Hutson kick)
Chi   Snyder 26yd FG
GB   Hinkle 1yd run (Huston kick)
Chi   Gallarneau 81yd punt return (kick blocked)
Chi   Snyder 24yd FG

SEASON: Bears 11-1-0 (1st)   Packers 10-2-0 (2nd)
          Beat Giants 37-9
          in title game

1942

9/27
Bears 44-28   City Stadium   20,007

This was the season opener for both teams and the highest scoring rivalry game to date. It was also one the testier battles, with the Bears penalized seven times for 102 yards. Chicago rallied for 17 points in the final six minutes to overtake the Packers. They capitalized on two Green Bay fumbles. Fullback Gary Famiglietti scored three touchdowns, and Packer quarterback Cecil Isbell was intercepted four times, twice by Clyde "Bulldog" Turner.

* On the Bears' bus ride from the Northland Hotel to the stadium, fans stopped the bus and nearly tipped it over.

Bears	7	6	14	17	44
Packers	0	21	7	0	28

Chi Nolting 38yd run (Stydahar kick)
GB   Brock 1yd run (Hutson kick)
Chi Wilson 2yd interception return (kick blocked)
GB   Hutson 40yd pass from Isbell (Hutson kick)
GB   Canadeo 1yd run (Hutson kick)
Chi Famiglietti 4yd run (Maznicki kick)
Chi Famiglietti 2yd run (Maznicki kick)
GB   Hutson 25yd pass from Isbell (Hutson kick)
Chi Maznicki 17yd FG
Chi Nolting 35yd fumble return (Artoe kick)
Chi Famiglietti 5yd run (Artoe kick)

....

11/15
Bears 38-7   Wrigley Field   42,787

By their second game of 1942, George Halas had rejoined the Navy. He appointed "Hunk" Anderson and Luke Johnsos as replacement co-coaches. The Bears still dominated their archrival, and they pushed the Packers around with 14 penalties for 118 yards. Green Bay was not penalized.

The intimidating Bears defense did not let the Packers offense get untracked. They held Green Bay to 43 yards rushing and 208 yards overall. The Bears T-formation offense generated 342 yards, even though the Packers claimed they knew how quarterback Sid Lukman tipped off his plays.

In 1942, Chicago beat their opponents by an average score of 34-7. Including the postseason, this was the Bears' 15th straight win. Their last loss was just over one year ago to Green Bay. They finished the 1942 regular season undefeated, and with this victory, they were now 29-4 since 1940 (including the postseason).

Packers   0   0   0   7   7
Bears   7 14 10   7   38
Chi Turner 42yd fumble return (Artoe kick)
Chi Luckman 54yd interception return (Artoe kick)
Chi Petty 2yd run (Frank Maznicki kick)
Chi Maznicki 28yd FG
Chi McLean 29yd pass from O'Rourke (Artoe kick)
Chi McLean 65yd pass from O'Rourke (Maznicki kick)
GB   Hutson 6yd pass from Isbell (Hutson kick)

SEASON: Bears 11-0-0 (1st)   Packers 8-2-1 (2nd)
         Lost to Redskins 14-6
              in title game

1943

9/26
Tie 21-21   **City Stadium**   **23,675**

Tony Canadeo not only ran for 99 yards, but he also threw a long touchdown pass to Don Hutson in the fourth quarter that tied the game. In a role reversal of sorts, Sid Luckman and the Bears threw the ball more effectively than Green Bay, and the Packers ran the ball more effectively than Chicago. With the scored tied and less than one minute remaining, Chicago's Bob Snyder's field goal attempt was blocked.

* *This was the rivalry game's first tie since 1928.*

* *After this game, Hunk Anderson convinced Bronco Nagurski to come out of retirement to help the Bears.*

Bears   7   0   7   7   21
Packers   0   7   7   7   21
Chi Geyer 8yd pass from Sid Luckman (Snyder kick)
GB   Fritsch 4yd run (Hutson kick)
GB   Comp 6yd run (Hutson kick)
Chi Clark 21yd pass from Luckman (Snyder kick)
Chi Osmanski 6yd run (Snyder kick)
GB   Hutson 37yd pass from Canadeo (Hutson kick)

11/7
Bears 21-7   **Wrigley Field**   **43,425**

The steady rain and the mud slowed down the Packers more than it did the Bears. Sid Luckman did all the damage for the Bears with two touchdowns passes and a touchdown run. After a fairly even first half, Luckman threw his second touchdown pass in the third quarter. In the fourth quarter, he marched the Bears 70 yards and put the game away with a short touchdown run. Chicago's 213 yards on the ground wore down the Packers who managed only one first down and one completion in the second half.

Packers 7 0 0 0 7
Bears   7 0 7 7 21
GB   Canadeo 20yd run (Hutson kick)
CHI McLean 66yd pass from Luckman (Snyder kick)
CHI Clark 38yd pass from Luckman (Snyder kick)
CHI Luckman 1yd run (Snyder kick)

SEASON: Bears 8-1-1 (1st)   Packers 7-2-1 (2nd)
              Beat Redskins 41-21
                  for the title

1944

9/24
Packers 42-28   **City Stadium**   **24,362**

This is the 50th game of the rivalry. Going into the game, the Bears led the series 26-18-5. In this one, the Packers won their first game at home over Chicago since 1939. In the first minutes of the game, Irv Comp threw a touchdown pass and ran for another to help get them out to a 19-0 lead. But with Sid Luckman on leave from the service to lead them, the Bears mounted a ferocious comeback.

Luckman threw three touchdowns and three interceptions. But it was Luckman's interception on *defense* that was called back due to a penalty that saved the day for Green Bay. The Packers scored on the next play, and they added the clincher on an interception return a short time later.

George Trafton, who battled the Packers as the Bears' center from 1920-1932, coached the Green Bay offensive line in 1944.

Bears   0   7   7 14   28
Packers 14 14   0 14   42
GB Brock 52yd pass from Comp (Hutson kick)
GB Comp 9yd run (Hutson kick)
GB Fritsch 1yd run (Hutson kick)
GB Hutson 26yd pass from Comp (Hutson kick)
Chi McLean 50yd lateral from Wilson/pass from Luckman (Gudauskas kick)
Chi Wilson 7yd pass from Luckman (Gudauskas kick)
Chi Wilson 3yd pass from Luckman (Gudauskas kick)
Chi Magarita 5yd run (Gudauskas kick)
GB Brock 42yd run (Hutson kick)
GB Fritsch 50yd interception return (Hutson kick)

....

11/5
Bears 21-0   Wrigley Field   45,553

Though nearly 3,000 fans Packer fans traveled south to see it, Green Bay lost its first game of the season. Home on a weekend pass once again, Sid Luckman had a great day for the Bears accounting for all three Chicago scores.

The Bears' defense picked off four Irv Comp passes and the Packers managed just 146 total yards of offense (49 on the ground). The Bears stopped Don Hutson's consecutive game scoring streak at 41, and the Packers were shutout for the first time since losing 2-0 to the Bears in 1938.

A fight took place between running backs Tony Canadeo of Green Bay and Chicago's Gary Famiglietti.

Packers 0 0 0 0 0
Bears 7 0 14 0 21
CHI Luckman 1 yard run (Gudauskas kick)
CHI McLean 31 yard pass from Luckman (Gudauskas kick)
CHI Wilson 24 yard pass from Luckman (Gudauskas kick)

SEASON: Bears 6-3-1 (2nd)   Packers 8-2-0 (1st)
Beat Giants 14-7
in title game

1945

9/30
Packers 31-21   **City Stadium**   **24,525**

After trailing 17-0, the Bears woke up in the second half. Gary Famiglietti scored three touchdowns for Chicago, but it proved to be too late. Though they outgained the Packers by over 100 yards, the Bears could not overcome their slow start and Green Bay's four rushing touchdowns.

* In the first play of the game, Lee Artoe punched Larry Craig in the face starting one of the most brutal periods of the rivalry.

Bears 0 0 7 14 21
Packers 10 0 7 14 31
GB Fritsch 7yd run (Hutson kick)
GB Fritsch 35yd FG
GB McKay 20yd run (Hutson kick)
CHI Famiglietti 3yd run (Gudauskas kick)
CHI Famiglietti 8 yd run (Gudauskas kick)
GB Fritsch 1yd run (Hutson kick)
CHI Famiglietti 3yd run (Gudauskas kick)
GB Perkins 2yd run (Hutson kick)

11/4
Bears 28-24   **Wrigley Field**   **45,527**

With the Bears were on the lookout for revenge for Lee Artoe's punch in the previous game, this was a vicious game. Two players were ejected, and Artoe was sent to the hospital with a broken jaw by Green Bay's Ken Keuper. From many reports, the referees let the game get out of control.

The winless Bears upset the defending champions with a great defensive effort. They held Green Bay to nine first downs (29 yards rushing) and 180 total yards (396 for Chicago). While the Bears fell behind 14-0, two long drives of 88 and 71 yards engineered by Luckman made it a game. After going in front, the Bears put it away with their powerful running game (271 yards).

This was the first losing season for the Bears since 1929.

Packers   14 10   0   0   24
Bears   0 21   7   0   28
GB   Goodnight 67 yd pass from Comp (Hutson kick)
GB   Comp 54yd interception return (Hutson kick)
CHI Margarita 2yd run (Pete Gudauskas kick)
GB   Craig 18yd fumble return (Hutson kick)
CHI Margarita 7yd run (Gudauskas kick)
GB   Fritsch 49yd field goal
CHI Kavanaugh 15yd pass fr om Luckman (Gudauskas kick)
CHI Fordham 1yd run (Gudauskas kick)

SEASON: Bears 3-7-0 (4th)   Packers 6-4-0 (3rd)

1946

9/29
Bears 30-7   **City Stadium**   **25,049**

In a bloody battle, the Packers' didn't complete a pass until the fourth quarter! Sid Luckman for Chicago didn't have that problem as he completed two touchdown passes to put the Bears in front early. A fumble by Tony Canadeo setup Luckman's second touchdown toss. In the third quarter, Canadeo was intercepted deep inside Packer territory. Chicago's Dick Schweidler scored on the next play to put Chicago up 24-0 and squash any hopes of a Packer comeback. The dominant Bears outgained Green Bay 432 to 114.

* On one play, Green Bay end Carl Mulleneaux suffered "five dislocated vertebrae, a concussion, a broken nose, facial cuts, and three broken teeth."[6] He never played again. Three other Packers left the game with injuries.

* Don Hutson's retirement ceremony took place at halftime. Because Hutson changed his mind so many times about retiring, Halas hung onto the defensive game plans he drew up for Hutson for several more years!

* A Packer fan shouted at Halas from the stands. Halas responded by admonishing the man's crude language!

Bears   3 14 7 6   30
Packers 0   0 0 7   7
Chi Maznicki 27 yd FG
Chi Kavanaugh 23yd pass from Luckman (Maznicki kick)
Chi McLean 33yd pass from Luckman (Maznicki kick)
Chi Schweidler 27 yd run (Maznicki kick)
Chi Osmanski 20yd run (Kick failed)
GB   McKay 9yd run (McKay kick)

....

11/3
Bears 10-7   Wrigley Field   46,321

This was a defensive battle with a scoreless first half. In the third quarter, Ted Fritsch's fumble was recovered by Chicago's Ed Sprinkle. Sprinkle, allegedly a dirty player who earned the moniker of *Meanest Man in Football*, picked up the fumble and rumbled 30 yards for a touchdown. With under a minute left, Fritsch tried to redeem himself with a touchdown run. But it was too late. The Bears had now won 11 of the last 15 rivalry games!

Before the game, the Bears' honored a teammate, Young Bussey, who was killed in the Philippines in March.

Packers   0   0   0   7   10
Bears   0   0 10 0   7
Chi   Sprinkle 30yd fumble return (Maznicki kick)
Chi   Maznicki 28yd FG
GB   Fritsch 3yd run (Fritsch kick)

SEASON: Bears 8-2-1 (1st)   Packers 6-5-0 (3rd)
　　　　　Beat Giants 24-14
　　　　　in title game

1947

9/28
Packers 29-20   City Stadium   25,461

In an amazing upset, the Packers defeated the defending champion Bears in the season opener. Using the T-Formation for the first time, Lambeau tried to light a spark under an offense that hadn't recovered from Don Hutson's retirement. Their new quarterback did exactly that with an inspiring performance. *Indian* Jack Jacobs threw for two touchdowns passes, ran for another and intercepted two passes on defense! Green Bay also ran for 246 yards and the defense intercepted five passes.

*ced * Rookie running back Don Kindt of the Bears arrived late to the game because the team doctor was late giving him a novocaine injection for his injured ankle. Kindt was locked out of the stadium and missed the first seven minutes of the game.*

Bears   6   7   0   7   20
Packers   3 14   2 10   29
GB   Cuff 28 yd FG
Chi   Fenimore 3yd run (kick blocked)
GB   Luhn 25yd pass from Jacobs (Cuff kick)

GB   Smith 36yd pass from Jacobs (Cuff kick)
CHI Keane 11yd pass from Luckman (McLean kick)
GB   Safety McAfee tackled in the end zone by Smith
GB   Cuff 25yd FG
Chi Keane 15yd pass from Luckman (McLean kick)
GB   Jacobs 1yd run (Cuff kick)

....

11/9
Bears 20-17   Wrigley Field   46,112

An appreciative crowd welcomed Jim Thorpe, the great Olympian, to the rivalry game. From 1920-21, Thorpe served as the first commissioner of the American Professional Players Association (APPA), the league that eventually became the NFL in 1921.

Chicago came back from 10 points down to earn a split in the season series. To preserve the win, the Bears put together two impressive goal line stands, and they blocked Ward Cuff's field goal attempt in the final minute of the game. There were 10 fumbles in this hard hitting battle and, the Bears prevailed despite turning the ball over nine times!

After one play, Ed "The Claw" Sprinkle of Chicago threw a Green Bay helmet downfield over the heads of the Packers.

Green Bay's phones and radios on the sidelines did not work. The Bears did not stop using their equipment as required by league rules. The Packers complained, but to no avail.

Packers   0   10   0   7   17
Bears   0   14   6   0   20
GB   Schlinkman 15 yard run (Cuff kick)
GB   Fritsch 50 yard FG
Chi Kavanaugh 81 yard pass from Luckman (McLean kick)
Chi Gallarneau 8 yard run (McLean kick)
Chi Osmanski 24 yard run (Kick failed)
GB   Forte 8 yard pass from Jacobs (Cuff kick)

SEASON: Bears 8-4-0 (2nd)   Packers 6-5-1 (3rd)

1948

9/26
Bears 45-7   **City Stadium**   **25,546**

Ouch! The Packers get pummeled. To date, this was the worst beating defeat that the Packers had ever suffered from their neighbors to the south. Chicago's three great quarterbacks – all-pro Sid Luckman and rookies Bobby Layne and Johnny Lujack – all administered the punishment.

In his first game in the NFL, Johnny Lujack scored the Bears' first touchdown, and he intercepted three passes. Each of the interceptions led to Bear touchdowns. Bobby Layne also shined with a touchdown pass to Ed Sprinkle in his debut. The Bears kept the ball away from Green Bay by running the ball 54 times for 240 yards! Green Bay ran just eight plays in the second half!

Packers Fans booed the home team after this game.

Bears   14 17 7 7   45
Packers   0   0   0 7   7
Chi   Lujack 3yd run (Fred Venturelli kick)
Chi   Mullins 33yd interception return (Venturelli kick)
Chi   Venturelli 12yd FG
Chi   McAfee 10yd run (Venturelli kick)
Chi   Holovak 10yd run (Venturelli kick)
Chi   Sprinkle, 1yd pass from Luckman (Venturelli kick)
GB   Schlinkman 1yd run (Cody kick)
Chi   Sprinkle 34yd pass from Layne (Venturelli kick)

....

11/14
Bears 7-6   **Wrigley Field**   **48,113**

After a scoreless first half, Chicago's young quarterback, Bobby Layne, threw a touchdown pass to the all-pro George McAfee to put the Bears in front. After Green Bay came back to score with three minutes left, Ed Cody missed the extra point to give the game to the Bears.

Sixteen flags were thrown for 150 yards!

Three thousand fans greeted the Packers when they came home.

```
Packers  0  0  0  6   6
Bears    0  0  7  0   7
```
Chi McAfee 34yd pass from Layne (Lawler kick)
GB   Luhn 13yd pass from Jacobs (kick failed)

SEASON: Bears 10-2-0 (2nd)   Packers 3-9-0 (4th)

1949

9/25
Bears 17-0   **City Stadium**   **25,571**

This was the last game Curly Lambeau would coach against the Bears as the head coach of the Green Bay Packers. Lambeau stepped aside after this game in order to devote more time to rebuilding the Packers and handling other responsibilities of a growing football operation.

Chicago shuts out Green Bay. Bears' quarterback Johnny Lujack was directly responsible for all of Chicago's points even though he had to receive several novocain injections for his separated shoulders (yes, both!). After a scoreless first half, Lujack's threw two touchdowns passes and kicked a field goal to put the Bears in front. The Chicago defense did not allow a completed pass all afternoon, and they intercepted four passes. Green Bay only got inside the Bears' 25 yard once all day.

The Bears' mascot was roughed-up during the game by Packer fans. That was the only battle that went Green Bay's way all day!

Lambeau's record against the Chicago was 21-34-5. Though this was the last game Lambeau physically coached, his record included a loss to Chicago later in the season.

```
Bears     0  0  3  14  17
Packers   0  0  0   0   0
```
Chi Lujack 16yd FG
Chi Boone 37yd pass from Lujack (Lujack kick)
Chi Kavanaugh 27yd pass from Lujack (Lujack kick)

....

11/6
Bears 24-3   **Wrigley Field**   **47,218**

Chicago swept the season series for the second year in a row. The game was decided in the fourth quarter when the Bears' Johnny Lujack broke it open with two long touchdown drives. Chicago's defense also stopped Green Bay when it counted. The Packers were inside the Bears' 20 yard four times but came away with only three points.

In a hero-like welcome after this loss, fans who met the train in Green Bay carried Tony Canadeo off the platform!

```
Packers   0  0  3   0   3
Bears     3  7  0  14  24
```
Chi Blanda 28yd FG
Chi Rykovich 1 yd run (Johnny Lujack kick)
GB   Ethridge 22yd FG
Chi Lujack 20yd run (Lujack kick)
Chi Rykovich 5yd run (Lujack kick)

SEASON: Bears 9-3-0 (2nd)   Packers 2-10-0 (5th)

Rivalry Stars of the 1940s

Sid Luckman   1939-50   QB/DB

Luckman played at Columbia where he was hand-picked by George Halas to be the quarterback of the Bears T-formation offense. He led Chicago to four NFL titles in the 1940s, not including the undefeated regular season of 1942. Luckman was the first NFL quarterback to throw for more than 400 yards in a game, and he was the league's MVP in 1943. Always a Halas favorite, Luckman coached with "Papa Bear" after his retirement and is still considered the greatest quarterback in Chicago Bear history.

Clyde "Bulldog" Turner   1940-52   C/LB

After graduating from Hardin-Simmons, Turner played 12 years in Chicago. He was an outstanding center who played every position on the offensive line. As a linebacker, in 1942, his eight interceptions led the league. Turner also intercepted four passes in five NFL championship games. After retiring, Turner coached the Bears' offensive line and he was the head coach of the New York Titans of the AFL in 1962.

Ken Kavanaugh   1940-50   DE

Ken Kavanaugh of LSU was a receiver for the Bears for eight years and a distinguished fighter pilot in World War II. Kavanaugh still holds the Bears' record for career touchdown receptions (50) and shares the record for touchdown catches in a single season with 13. After playing for the Bears, Kavanaugh spent 45 years as an assistant coach and scout for the New York Giants.

☆

Ted Fritsch   1942-50   FB

Fritsch starred at UW-Stevens Point and then played for the "hometown" Packers. He led Green Bay in rushing three times, and, along with Tony Canadeo, provided the one-two punch of the Green Bay offense in the mid-to-late forties. He scored both of Green Bay's touchdowns in the 1944 NFL Championship Game. Fritsch also led the league in scoring in 1946.

Tony Canadeo   1941-44, 1946-52   B, DB

The Grey Ghost of Gonzaga, Canadeo could run, pass, punt and return kicks. He led the Packers in rushing five times, including in 1949 when he was the first 1,000 yard rusher in Packer history. In the late 1940s, he was consistently among the league leaders in yards, attempts and yards per carry. After retiring, Canadeo called Packer games on the radio and he was a member of the Executive Committee. His #3 is one of only five numbers retired by the franchise.

Larry Craig   1939-49   RB, DE

On offense, Craig was a great blocker who led the way for Hinkle and Canadeo. His was a good defensive end which allowed the Packers to move Don Hutson to safety. In 1941, Craig was one of the first players fined by the NFL (for fighting). On September 30, 1945, Craig was hit hard in the face by Chicago's Lee Artoe which set off one of the most nasty periods of the rivalry.

> *"Through the years, play on the field was always rougher than any other game when the two teams met. It has not been unusual to have a large number of broken bones, twisted ankles, poked eyes, missing teeth and players from both sides knocked senseless and unconscious."*[16]

The Games
1950-59
Wins

Bears 14   1 Tie   Packers 5

Series: 49-26-6 Bears

Growth was the nation's mantra in the fifties and the NFL followed suit. The league expanded to three new cities when it absorbed teams from the rival All-America Football Conference – the Cleveland Browns, Baltimore Colts and the San Francisco Forty-Niners. Right from the start, the Browns surprisingly overpowered everyone on their way to six straight Eastern Conference titles and three NFL championships.

When *free substitution* became permanent in 1950, the league exploded in new talent. Players no longer had to play both offense and defense. Talented players in one skill area (kicking, catching etc.) could now play in the NFL. Rosters were expanded. More speed, skill and spectacular play brought attention to the pro game like never before. The 1951 title game was the first national television broadcast of an NFL game and fans began watching in record numbers. Some teams even blacked-out home games to protect ticket sales. In 1958, *The Greatest Game Ever Played* between the Colts and the Giants captivated the nation, and pro football and television were on their way to unimaginable popularity together.

The rivalry game continued to be beyond brutal. At times, the games became more about settling scores than scoring points. Occasionally, even the fans even got involved. When they played in Green Bay, Halas warned the Bears to wear their helmets on the bench to protect against flying bottles and cans.

In the fifties, the Bears made it to the '56 championship game but they lost to the Giants. The Packers never got close to making it to a title game and were clearly the league's doormat. For many, Green Bay had become a relic of pro football's past, a tiny outpost destined to fail in the modern NFL. Few players wanted to play in the *salt mines of Siberia* and owners groused that the Packers should move to inject new life and a new stadium into the moribund franchise. But in 1957, Green Bay built a new stadium, and in 1959, they hired a new coach – Vince Lombardi. The rivalry game then entered an unforgettable era.

1950

10/1
Packers 31-21   City Stadium   24,893

A big win for Packers' new coach, Gene Ronzani, a former Chicago Bear player and assistant coach. Green Bay came from behind in an exciting second half to defeat the heavily favored Bears.

Trailing 7-3 at halftime, the Packers put together a string of explosive plays in the third quarter for a thrilling comeback. They picked off two Johnny Lujack passes and returned them for touchdowns. Billy Grimes' electrifying 68 yard punt return brought six more. By the start of the fourth quarter, they led 24-14. The teams traded touchdowns in the fourth quarter, with veteran quarterback Sid Luckman leading Chicago's touchdown drive.

The Bears dominated the statistical battle with 400 total yards compared to Green Bay's 233. They also held the Packers to just eight first downs.

* *Packers' center Clayton Tonnemaker was ejected for fighting.*

Bears   0 7   7 7   21
Packers   3 0 21 7   31
GB   Fritsch 20yd FG
Chi Rykovich 1yd run (Lujack kick)
GB   Dryer 28yd interception return (Fritsch kick)
GB   Steiner 94yd interception return (Fritsch kick)
Chi Lujack 1yd (Lujack kick)
GB   Grimes 68yd punt return (Fritsch kick)
GB   Reid 5yd pass from Christman (Fritsch kick)
Chi Rykovich 2yd run (Lujack kick)

....

10/15
Bears 28-14   Wrigley Field   51,065

Billy Grimes' explosive kickoff return right in front of the Green Bay bench put the Packers in front. After that, it was all Johnny Lujack and the Bears. Lujack got revenge for the interceptions he threw two weeks ago by scoring three times in this game!

A 7-7 first half had Green Bay hoping to pull off another upset. But five minutes into the third quarter, Harper Davis scored for Chicago. Minutes later, Lujack scored his second touchdown to effectively close the door on any possible comeback. Green Bay's offense cooperated with three turnovers and 11 punts!

Four thousand Packer fans attended this game.

Packers 7 0   0 7   14
Bears   0 7 14 7   28
GB   Grimes 73yd run (Fritsch kick)
CHI Lujack 25yd run (Lujack kick)
CHI Davis 36yd run (Lujack kick)
CHI Lujack 1 yd run (Lujack kick)
CHI Lujack 8yd run (Lujack kick)
GB   Reid 14yd run (Fritsch kick)

SEASON: Bears 9-3-0 (2nd)   Packers 3-9-0 (5th)

1951

9/30
Bears 31-20   **City Stadium**   **24,666**

The Packers unveil Coach Ronzani's new offensive formation – the shotgun – and it had some success. Green Bay relied heavily on the pass in 1951, and this game started it all. They passed 41 times, completed 22 and scored two aerial touchdowns. But the Bears' defense refused to break. With Green Bay unable to generate much of a running attack (68 yards) their reliance on the pass was costly. Two key interceptions by Chicago's sensational rookie Gene Schroeder put an end to Green Bay's chances.

Penalty Yardage.....Bears > 114 yards.....Packers > 109 yards

Whizzer White, who scored the first touchdown for Chicago, was a United States Supreme Court Justice from 1962-1993!

On the trip home, George Halas was punched by a Packer fan at the train station. Halas ran after the fan after he was hit!

Bears   10   7   7   7   31
Packers   0   6   7   7   20
Chi White 8yd run (Lujack kick)
Chi Blanda 46yd FG
Chi Rykovich 1yd run (Lujack kick)
GB   Mann 12yd pass from Thomason (kick failed)
Chi Dottley 1yd run (Lujack kick)
GB   Cloud 1yd pass from Thomason (Cone kick)
Chi Hunsinger 5yd run (Lujack kick)
GB   Cloud 1yd run (Cone kick)

11/18
Bears 24-13   **Wrigley Field**   **36,771**

This time around, the Packers tried their new shotgun formation with the fullback lined up as a receiver. Green Bay led at halftime, and they appeared to have the Bears' number. But Chicago won the critical third quarter. With Green Bay driving deep in Bears' territory, Chicago linebacker George Connor hit Green Bay quarterback Tobin Rote so hard that he fumbled. The Bears recovered, and Johnny Lujack led them on an 89 yard drive that put them in front to stay.

* Rote ran for 150 yards. For the season, he set a Packer quarterback record that still stands for average rushing yardage in a season (6.88 yards).*

* Packer receiver Dom Moselle crashed into Wrigley Field's brick wall chasing down a pass from Rote.*

* Freezing temperatures silenced the Packers' Lumberjack Band.*

```
Packers   0  13   0   0   13
Bears     3   7   7   7   24
```
Chi   Blanda 3yd FG
GB   Moselle 5yd run (Cone kick)
GB   Canadeo 10yd pass from Rote (Kick failed)
Chi   Romanik 1yd run (Blanda kick)
Chi   Gulyanics 3 yard run (Blanda kick)
Chi   Rykovich 1 yard run (Blanda kick)

SEASON: Bears 7-5-0 (4th)   Packers 3-9-0 (5th)

1952

9/28
Bears 24-14   **City Stadium**   **24,656**

Numbers were painted on the field for the first time, and the Bears came from behind to beat Green Bay. After George Blanda missed three consecutive field goals, the Bears finally got on the board when Wizzer White put one through the uprights from the 30 yard line. A blocked punt by John Martinkovic led to Green Bay's touchdown and a 7-3 halftime lead.

The second half was all Chicago. The turning point came in the fourth quarter when Ed Sprinkle blocked a Green Bay field goal attempt. The Bears recovered at midfield, and they capitalized with the go-ahead touchdown. A short time later, a Packer fumble led to another Chicago touchdown. The Bears outgained the Packers (378-210) and the Green Bay turned the ball over four times.

* Twenty-one penalties were called for 186 yards. In the last three games, the teams were penalized for over 600 yards!

Bears   3 0 7 14   24
Packers 0 7 0 7   14
Chi   White 30yd FG
GB   Rote 5yd run (Cone kick)
Chi   Dottley 25yd pass from Williams (Blanda kick)
Chi   Schroeder 16yd pass from Williams (Blanda kick)
GB   Howton 39yd pass from Rote (Cone kick)

....

11/9
Packers 41-28   Wrigley Field   41,751

The Packers generated nearly 400 yards of offense in this rematch. On Green Bay' the opening drive, both quarterbacks, Tobin Rote and Babe Parrilli, played . Rote ran it. Parilli threw it. It worked with Parilli connecting with Billy Howton for an early Packer lead.

Green Bay fullback Fred Cone then took over. The young Packer scored the next 17 points converting on a short run, a long touchdown pass and a field goal. He also kicked the extra points. Long kickoff returns kept Chicago close, but they couldn't keep up with Green Bay (390-164 total yards). It was an emotional win for the Packers who hadn't won at Wrigley since 1941.

* Six thousand fans greeted their heroes at the North Western Train Station.

* This is just the second time since 1929 that the Bears finsihed with a losing record.

Packers 7 10 7 17   41
Bears   7   0 7 14   28
GB   Howton 19 yard pass from Parilli (Cone kick)
Chi Campbell 86 yd kickoff return (Blanda kick)
GB   Cone 1yd run (Cone kick)
GB   Cone 12yd FG
GB   Cone 37yd pass from Rote (Cone kick)
Chi Macon 89yd kickoff return (Blanda kick)
GB   Martinkovic recovers fumble in end zone (Cone kick)
GB   Reichardt 37yd FG
GB   Mann 27yd pass from Parilli (Cone kick)
Chi Schroeder 48yd pass from Romanik (Blanda kick)
Chi Morrison 12yd pass from Romanik (Blanda kick)

SEASON: Bears 5-7-0 (5th)   Packers 6-6-0 (4th)

1953

10/4
Bears 17-13   City Stadium   24,835

A turnover-prone contest (five for Green Bay and four for Chicago) went the Bears' way after, surprise, a Packer fumble in the fourth quarter. This game was also a nasty game with 15 penalty flags for 135 yards.

With under four minutes to play and a 13-10 lead, the Packers fumbled on the Bears' two yard line. The Bears recovered and capitalized. Quarterback George Blanda led a long drive that culminated with his winning touchdown pass to end Jim Dooley, future coach of the Bears!

Bears   3 7 0   7   17
Packers 6 7 0   0   13
Chi Blanda 40yd FG
GB   Mann 19yd pass from Rote (kick failed)
GB   Dawson 60yd punt return (Cone kick)
Chi Dottley 2yd run (Blanda kick)
Chi Dooley 16yd pass from Blanda (Blanda kick)

11/8
TIE 21-21   **Wrigley Field**   **39,889**

In a game of big plays, Bobby Dillon of Green Bay picked off an early George Blanda pass and went 49 yards for a touchdown. Fred Cone then exploded 41 yards off tackle to put the Packers in command.

The Bears then grabbed an interception of their own and returned it for a touchdown. Blanda then threw two touchdown passes to give the Bears the lead by the fourth quarter. With two minutes left, Babe Parilli then led the Packers back on an 80 yard march to tie the game!

* *Halas offered $50 to any player who could knock the "mustache" off of Bob Mann's face. Mann was the Packers' only black player.*

Packers 14 0 0 7   21
Bears   7 7 0 7   21
GB   Dillon 49yd interception return (Cone kick)
GB   Cone 41yd run (Cone kick)
Chi Kindt 67yd interception return (George Blanda kick)
Chi Dooley 33yd pass from Blanda (Blanda kick)
Chi Hoffman 14yd pass from Blanda (Blanda kick)
GB   Howton 23yd pass from Parilli (Cone kick)

SEASON: Bears 3-8-1 (4th)   Packers 2-9-1 (6th)

1954

10/3
Bears 10-3   **City Stadium**   **24,414**

Three inches of rain and a muddy field greeted Green Bay's new coach Lisle Blackbourn in his first rivalry game. Ten turnovers, five by each squad, also had to have him

Though it was a scoreless first half, each team moved the ball without too much difficuty, Green Bay finally got on the board with a third quarter field goal. A fumble recovery in the fourth quarter by former

Packer Paul "Big Daddy" Lipscomb gave the Bears the ball at the Green Bay nine. Moments later, George Blanda found Billy Stone in the end zone to put the Bears in front. Blanda's toe clinched it a short time later.

After the game, Halas complained about the conditions of the field. He said he expected more from a professional football franchise.

```
Bears     0   0   0   10   10
Packers   0   0   3   0    3
```
GB   Cone 40yd FG
Chi   Stone 5yd pass from Blanda (Blanda kick)
Chi   Blanda 23yd FG

....

11/7
Bears 28-23   **Wrigley Field**   **47,038**

Twenty-three unanswered points, including two touchdowns by Packer rookie Max McGee, didn't deter the Bears. Determined quarterback George Blanda was the hero with a touchdown pass to start the game and another one with 2:05 left in the fourth quarter to win it.

With the Packers leading 16-14, Max McGee appeared to put the game away for Green Bay with his second touchdown catch. The 23-14 lead vanished, however, after a Packer fumble was returned for a touchdown and George Blanda engineered another scoring drive for the Bears late in the quarter. Green Bay quarterback Tobin Rote, who broke his nose earlier in the game, was sacked on Chicago's 16 yard line as time ran out.

Veryl Switzer's 93 yard punt return was the longest in Packer history until Steve Odom's 95 yarder in 1974 (also against the Bears).

```
Packers   0   13   3   7    23
Bears     7   7    0   14   28
```
Chi   Dooley 40yd pass from Blanda (Blanda kick)
Chi   Jagade 2yd run (Blanda kick)
GB   McGee 4yd pass from Rote (Cone kick)
GB   Switzer 93yd punt return (kick failed)
GB   Cone 30yd FG

GB McGee 37yd pass from Rote (Cone kick)
Chi Hansen 35yd fumble return (Blanda kick)
Chi Hoffman 7yd pass from Blanda (Blanda kick)

SEASON: Bears 8-4-0 (2nd)   Packers 4-8-0 (5th)

1955

10/2
Packers 24-3 — City Stadium — 24,662

Even though some thought that Green Bay would be no match for the Bears, six turnovers by Chicago – four in the fourth quarter – helped Green Bay to an easy win. The Packers started the season 2-0 for the first time since 1947. Tobin Rote had one of his most-memorable games in a Packer uniform with two touchdown passes and a touchdown run. Packer fullback Howie Ferguson also bulled his way through the Chicago defense for 153 of the Packers' 223 yards on the ground.

Before the season, Halas announced his retirement effective at the end of the year.

Bears   0   0   3   0   3
Packers   0 10   7   7   24
GB Cone 24yd FG
GB Howton 32yd pass from Rote (Cone kick)
Chi Blanda 47yd FG
GB Rote 1yd run (Cone kick)
GB Knafelc 23yd pass from Rote (Cone kick)

....

11/6
Bears 52-31 — Wrigley Field — 48,890

The Bears split the season series with the highest scoring game in the rivalry's history. The score, however, did not accurately reflect how dominant the Bears were. A better indicator was the 38-3 lead that the Bears had at the start of the fourth quarter. Five Packer fumbles also helped Chicago pound the Packers for 406 yards on the ground and 504 yards overall. The Bears were so dominant that they never had to punt!

On a kickoff return, Veryl Switzer of Green Bay was hit so hard by George Conner that some fans and players thought he was dead. For six weeks, Switzer spit up blood every time he was hit.

Packers   0   3   0   28   31
Bears   14 14 10   14   52
Chi   Jagade 42yd run (Blanda kick)
Chi   Watkins 13yd run (Blanda kick)
Chi   Watkins 29yd run (Blanda kick)
GB   Cone 41yd FG
Chi   Casares 2yd run (Blanda kick)
Chi   Hill 14yd pass from Brown (Blanda kick)
Chi   Blanda 38yd FG
Chi   McColl 24yd pass from Bob Williams (Blanda kick)
GB   Howton 27yd pass from Rote (Cone kick)
GB   Ferguson 1yd run (Cone kick)
Chi   Drzewiscki 11yd run (Blanda kick)
GB   Ferguson 1yd run (Cone kick)
GB   Rote 1 yd run (Cone kick)

SEASON: Bears 8-4-0 (2nd)   Packers 6-6-0 (3rd)

1956

10/7
Bears 37-21   **City Stadium**   **24,668**

John "Paddy" Driscoll, a former star quarterback for the Bears in the twenties, was Chicago's he new coach. Ed Brown starred in this game for Chicago with two touchdown passes and a fumble recovery for a score! Rick Casares ran for 139 yards, and the Bears ran all over the Packers for 278 yards. George Blanda kicked three field goals, and he set a record with four extra points, giving him 150 without a miss.

This was the last Bear-Packer game played at the original City Stadium. It was televised in Green Bay by CBS and called by broadcaster Ray Scott. The old stadium, which hosted 32 games between the rivals, had to be replaced to keep the Packers competitive in the growing NFL.

Harold Carmichael's 106 yard kickoff return was an exciting farewell to the old stadium. It remains a Packer record.

Bears   10 10   7 10   37
Packers   7   7   0   7   21
Chi   Casares 9yd pass from Brown (Blanda kick)
GB   Carmichael 106yd kickoff return (Cone kick) T
Chi   Blanda 29yd FG
Chi   Blanda 41yd FG
GB   Howton 6yd pass from Rote (Cone kick)
Chi   Brown 3yd fumble return (Blanda kick)
Chi   Casares 14yd run (Blanda kick)
GB   Howton 16 yard pass from Rote (Cone kick)
Chi   Blanda 11yd FG
Chi   McColl 9yd pass from Brown (Blanda kick)

....

11/11
Bears 38-14   Wrigley Field   49,172

The 75th game of the rivalry saw another dominant performance by the Bears. They went 72 yards on their opening drive to set the pace, and the Packers never came close to keeping up. They put the game away quickly in the second quarter when quarterback George Blanda threw two of his three touchdown bombs to put Chicago in front by 21.

The 1956 version of the *Monsters of the Midway* blew through the Packers' defense for 494 total yards! They harrassed Packer quarterback Tobin Rote all game. He threw three interceptions, one of which was returned 52 yards for a touchdown by J.C. Caroline. Not a good day for Green Bay.

This was the first rivalry game televised back in Green Bay.

After catching a touchdown, Packers' Gary Kanflac crashed into the brick wall at Wrigley along the right field line.

```
Packers  0   7  7  0  14
Bears    7  21  7  3  38
```
Chi Hoffman 5yd run (Blanda kick)
Chi Hill 23yd pass from Blanda (Blanda kick)
Chi McColl 69yd pass from Blanda (Blanda kick)
GB   Knafelc 23yd pass from Rote (Cone kick)
Chi Caroline 52yd interception return (Blanda kick)
GB   Howton 49yd pass from Rote (Cone kick)
Chi Hill 70 yd pass from Blanda (Blanda kick)
Chi Blanda 29yd FG

SEASON: Bears 9-2-1 (1st)   Packers 4-8-0 (5th)
             Lost to Giants 47-7
               in title game

1957

9/29
Packers 21-17   **City Stadium**   **32,132**

This is the first game ever played in *new* City Stadium. It was the first stadium built exclusively for football, and in 1965, it was renamed Lambeau Field in honor of Packer founder Curly Lambeau.

The game was a see-saw battle that was helped along by ten turnovers, six for Chicago and four for Green Bay. The Bears scored after a long touchdown drive, and Babe Parilli, who Green Bay had just reacquired, countered with his first scoring pass of the day. After trading two more touchdowns, the game was even at halftime.

In the third quarter, the Packers forced the Bears to settle for a field goal from the 13 yard line. That stop made the difference. Parilli connected with Gary Knaflec with eight minutes left in the game for what proved to be the winner.

* *The opening of new City Stadium was a city-wide party during a beautiful fall weekend. Festivities were held at old City Stadium and on the Fox River. The parade, which included a float from the Bears, attracted 70,000 people!*

* *This was the first rivalry game televised back in Chicago.*

Bears   7 7 3 0   17
Packers 0 14 0 7   21
Chi Brown 5yd run (Blanda kick)
GB   Howton 37yd pass from Parilli (Cone kick)
Chi Hill 11yd pass from Brown (Blanda kick)
GB   Cone 1yd run (Cone run)
Chi Blanda 13yd FG
GB   Knaflec 6yd pass from Parilli (Cone kick)

....

11/10
Bears 21-14   **Wrigley Field**   **47,183**

In one of the rivalry's most controversial games, a third quarter touchdown pass from Bart Starr to Joe Johnson was ruled incomplete. The Green Bay bench nearly self-destructed. In a tense 14-14 tie in fourth quarter, the Bears embarked on an impressive 58 yard drive. Rookie Willie Galimore made two key catches on the drive, and Rick Casares scored his second touchdown of the day to win it with 1:01 remaining!

* *Also in the third quarter, Doug Atkins of the Bears punched Green Bay's guard Jim Salsbury. There was no ejection or penalty.*

Packers 7 7 0 0   14
Bears   7 7 0 7   21
Chi Casares 16 yard run (Blanda kick)
GB   Howton 47yd pass from Starr (Cone kick)
GB   McIlhenny 28yd pass from Starr (Cone kick)
Chi Hill 35yd pass from Bratkowski (Blanda kick)
Chi Casares 9yd run (Blanda kick)

SEASON: Bears 5-7-0 (5th)   Packers 3-9-0 (6th)

1958

9/28
Bears 34-20　　　　**City Stadium**　　　　32,150

George Halas returned to the sidelines to win another NFL title. In his return to Green Bay, he defeated his former halfback Ray "Scooter" McClean. McClean became Green Bay's third coach in nine years, and he presided over the worst season in Packer history.

The season began with the rivalry game. Despite the exciting interception return by Bobby Dillion in the first minute for the Packers, Willie Galimore of the Bears proved to be too much. His two rushing touchdowns in the first half helped stake the Bears to a 21-13 halftime lead. When quarterback Ed Brown found him in the third quarter with a 73 yard touchdown bomb, it put the game away.

The Bears had five sacks.

Bears　　7　14　7　6　34
Packers　10　3　0　7　20
GB　Dillon 37yd interception return (Hornung kick)
Chi　Galimore 1yd run (Blanda kick)
GB　Hornung 23yd FG
Chi　Galimore 8yd run (Blanda kick)
Chi　Brown 2yd run (Blanda kick)
GB　Hornung 30yd FG
Chi　Galimore 79yd pass from Brown (Blanda kick)
Chi　Hill 13yd pass from Brown (kick failed)
GB　Hornung 2yd run (Hornung kick)

....

11/9
Bears 24-10　　　　**Wrigley Field**　　　　48,424

After getting annihilated by the Colts the previous week 56-0, the Packers continued their losing ways. Chicago's defense controlled the game, and fullback Rick Casares (113 yards) was their offensive star.

Cornerback Jack Johnson's interception set up Chicago's first touchdown. After a 7-3 first half, the Bears struck twice in the third quarter. Rick Casares galloped for a long touchdown run, and Bill George forced a Bart Starr fumble in the end zone for the other. Chicago gave up only 145 total yards, and they recorded six sacks. In his first year back, "Papa Bear" swept Green Bay!

The names of Paul Hornung and Max McGee appeared in Chicago newspapers the following day for their night on the town after the game.

Packers 3 0 0 7   10
Bears   0 7 14 3   24
GB   Hornung 56yd FG
Chi Galimore 5yd run (Blanda kick)
Chi Casares 64yd run (Blanda kick)
Chi Bishop recovered fumble in the end zone (Blanda kick)
Chi Blanda 20yd field goal
GB   Taylor 3yd run (Hornung kick)

SEASON: Bears 8-4-0 (2nd)   Packers 1-10-1 (6th)

1959

9/27
Packers 9-6   City Stadium   32,150

New Green Bay coach Vince Lombardi faced the Bears in his first game *ever* as a head coach. He closed practices the week before the game to focus his new team.

Rain made it a physical game in the trenches with twice as many running plays as passing (78-37). The Bears led 6-0 in the fourth quarter on the strength of two long John Aveni field goals. With eight minutes left, Richie Pettibon fumbled a punt that was recovered by the Packers' Jim Ringo at the Bears' 26 yard line. Hornung and Taylor took it from there, and the Packers took the lead 7-6.

With five minutes left, Max McGee's 61 yard punt pinned Chicago at their two yard line. When quarterback Ed Brown was sacked on the next play by Dave Hanner and other in the end zone, the safety clinched Lombardi's first victory.

Total Yards: Bears 262   Packers 164.

```
Bears      0   3   0   3    6
Packers    0   0   0   9    9
```
Chi Aveni 46yd FG
Chi Aveni 42yd FG
GB Taylor 5yd run (Hornung kick)
GB Safety, Hanner sacked Brown in end zone

....

11/8
Bears 28-17   Wrigley Field   46,205

Two fumbles by Paul Hornung in the first quarter were converted into touchdowns by the Bears who led at halftime 21-10. In the third quarter, future Packer backup Zeke Bratkowski took off on a 42 yard scramble that led to the clinching touchdown. The Bears controlled the game with 172 yards on the ground. With the exception of a last minute punt return, Chicago kept Green Bay out of the end zone in the second half.

This was one of Paul Hornung's worst days as a Packer. He ran the ball four times for -3 yards. He also fumbled three times.

```
Packers   0   10   0   7    17
Bears     14   7   7   0    28
```
Chi Douglas 5yd run (Aveni kick)
Chi Casares 5yd run (Aveni kick)
GB Taylor 10yd run (Hornung kick)
GB Hornung 27yd FG
Chi Hill 36yd pass from Ed Brown (Aveni kick)
Chi Dooley 8yd pass from Bratkowski (Aveni kick)
GB Butler 61yd punt return (Hornung kick)

SEASON: Bears 8-4-0 (2nd)   Packers 7-5-0 (3rd)

Rivalry Stars of the 1950s

Bill George　　　1952-65　　　　　MLB

George was one of the toughest, and most beloved, Bears of all-time. He was a champion college wrestler at Wake Forest, before he played for Chicago. In 1954, he became the first in a long line of great middle linebackers for the Bears. George captained the Bears' defense for many years, and he was first team All-Pro for seven straight seasons. He was a leader of the defense that won the 1963 NFL title, and #61 has been retired by the Bears.

Rick Casares　　　1955-64　　　　　FB

After playing at Florida for three years, Casares was drafted into the Army. Halas liked him so much that he selected Casares as a *future* pick in 1954. Casares was a powerful runner who was the strength of the Bears' running game for a decade. He led the Bears in rushing six times and he topped the league once (1956). He was the Bears all-time leading rusher until Walter Payton arrived.

Doug Atkins　　　1955-66　　　　　E

Atkins was 6'8" and 285 pounds. He played at Tennessee before being drafted by Cleveland. Atkins was traded to the Bears in 1955 where his career really took off. Though he had a testy relationship with Halas, he took his anger out on opposing quarterbacks and running backs. He was a great pass rusher, strong against the run, and a four time first team all pro.

☆

Tobin Rote　　　1950-56　　　　　QB

After graduating from Rice, Tobin Rote became the Packers' starting quarterback as a rookie. In seven seasons, he was a dual threat with outstanding running ability and a great arm. A rugged and strong athlete, Rote was the greatest running quarterback in Packer history. He *led* Green Bay in rushing three times. In 1956, the year before he was traded to the Lions, Rote led the NFL in pass attempts, completions, passing yardage and touchdowns.

Bobby Dillon　　　　　1952-59　　　　　　　S

Out of Texas, Dillon played defensive back for Green Bay despite being blind in his left eye. He was one of the best safeties of his day and he is still the Packers' all-time interceptions leader with 52. Dillon also shares the Packer record with for four interceptions in a game. He played in four Pro Bowls, and he is a member of the all-time Packer team that was selected in 1969.

Billy Howton　　　　　1952-58　　　　　　　E

A two sport star at Rice (football and track), Dillon was a second round pick by Green Bay in 1952. He led the Packers in receiving for six straight seasons, and he was a four-time pro bowler. He played a major role in the player's union, and some suspected that this was the reason he was traded to Cleveland in 1959.

The Games
1960-69
Wins

Bears 5   Packers 15

Series: 54-41-6 Bears

Pro football's popularity picked up steam in the sixties! Teams began play in Minnesota, Miami, Atlanta, New Orleans and Cincinnati. Attendance was up, television ratings soared, and salaries were going through the roof. Teams began taking planes instead of trains, and the Packers no longer needed the spirited civic events to boost popularity or ticket sales. In the sixties, pro football became king.

When the NFL initially decided not to expand in 1959, several businessmen formed the American Football League (AFL). Teams were originally located in New York, Boston, Buffalo, Dallas, Los Angeles Oakland, Houston and Denver. A six-year war began between the leagues as they out spent each other for players and franchises. Fans enjoyed the new league's more exciting game. AFL teams threw early and often. The two leagues finally called a cease fire and merged on June 8, 1966. The first Super Bowl kicked off at the end of the 1966 season and, in many ways, today's NFL was born.

The sixties was very different decade for the Bears and the Packers. Green Bay couldn't have been more successful – five titles in seven years. Though Chicago won it all in 1963, Halas had difficulty keeping-up with Lombardi. Green Bay's success annoyed Halas and spiked his paranoia. He always kept one eye on the windows and rooftops when the Bears practiced in Green Bay, always looking for spies.

In 1960, after 23 ballots, Pete Rozelle, an executive with the Los Angeles Rams, was elected NFL commissioner following the death of Bert Bell. Rozelle led the league through its merger with the AFL and through explosive growth in popularity. As the seventies dawned, pro football was unquestionably America's game.

1960

9/25
Bears 17-14   **City Stadium**   **32,150**

This loss had Packer fans wondering right away if the team's success the year before was just an illusion. A scoreless first quarter gave way to 14 Green Bay points thanks to Jim Taylor and Paul Hornung. But the Bears struck quickly near the end of the fourth quarter. Willie Galimore began the comeback with a touchdown run. Taylor then fumbled on the Packers' next possession, and the Bears had their opportunity. They capitalized with Rick Casares' touchdown run. Then with three minutes left, Earl Legget intercepted a batted Bart Starr pass at the Green Bay 32 yard line. With 35 seconds left, John Aveni's toe finished off Green Bay.

* *Due to rain and a high school football game, George Halas was upset about the condition of the field.*

* *Green Bay completed just nine passes all day, and three Packer touchdowns were called back because of penalties*

Bears   0   0   0   17   17
Packers 0   7   7   0   14
GB   Taylor 1yd run (Hornung kick)
GB   Hornung 2yd run (Hornung kick)
Chi   Galimore 18yd run (Aveni kick)
Chi   Casares 26yd run (Aveni kick)
Chi   Aveni 16yd FG

12/4
Packers 41-13   Wrigley Field   46,406

Vince Lombardi's first win at Wrigley! In his seven years in Green Bay, the Packers dominated the Bears like never before. They won 12 of 15 games, and the Halas-Lombardi rivalry developed an intensity that at times belied the good friendship they shared.

In the biggest game of the season, defensive end Willie Davis blocked a punt to put up six for Green Bay. Bart Starr was 17 of 23 and he tossed two touchdown. Paul Hornung broke Don Hutson's single season scoring record (138) with 23 points giving him 152. Jim Taylor's 140 yards on the ground helped the Packers roll over the Bears and into a three way tie for first place with two games left.

* It was a very emotional game for the Packers. Jack Vainisi, Vince Lombardi's trusted scout and personnel assistant, died suddenly the week of the game. Vainisi was from Chicago and had drafted most of the Packer players. Lombardi and the players dedicated the game to him.

* Hornung flipped the football into the stands after scoring his second touchdown. It angered Halas. Lombardi promised to pay for the ball if Halas demanded it. The flip is considered the first end zone celebration!

* This is just the second win for the Packers in Chicago since 1941.

Packers 0 13 14 14   41
Bears   0   6   7   0   13
GB   Hornung 21yd FG
GB   Davis recovered a blocked punt in the end zone (Hornung kick)
Chi Dewveall 19yd pass from Brown (Kick blocked)
GB   Hornung 41yd FG
GB   Hornung 17 yd pass from Starr (Hornung kick)
GB   Taylor 2yd run (Hornung kick)
Chi Dooley 20yd pass from Bratkowski (Aveni kick)
GB   Hornung 10yd run (Hornung kick)
GB   McGee 46yd pass from Starr (Hornung kick)

Season: Bears 5-6-1 (5th)   Packers 8-4-0 (1st)
                                Lost to Eagles 17-13
                                in title game

1961

10/1
Packers 24-0   **City Stadium**   **38,669**

Green Bay's fullback Jim Taylor ran all over the Bears for 130 yards. He scored a touchdown and also set up a Paul Hornung field goal with the longest run of his career (53 yards). The Packers picked off four Chicago passes (two by Dan Currie) to stop any scoring threats. The Bears tried to disrupt the Packer offense by blitzing quarterback Bart Starr often, but he still threw for two touchdowns.

The last time the Packers shutout the Bears was in 1935.

Despite surgery to remove his appendix on 9/19, Packer defensive tackle Dave Hanner played in this game.

Bears   0   0   0   0   0
Packers   7   3   7   7   24
GB   Dowler 18yd pass from Starr (Hornung kick)
GB   Hornung 37yd FG
GB   Taylor 3yd run (Hornung kick)
GB   Kramer 17yd pass from Starr (Hornung kick)

....

11/12
Packers 31-28   **Wrigley Field**   **49,711**

The Bears scored first, but after that, the Packers put up 31 unanswered points. Bart Starr threw three touchdown passes. Army-bound Paul Hornung ran for one touchdown and caught another. He scored for 19 points in all. The Packers looked ready to sail home with 31-7 lead in the third quarter.

The Bears suprisingly roared back on the shoulders of Mike Ditka. Ditka caught nine passes for 190 yards. His second and third touchdown catches brought the Bears back in the second half. The Packers withstood the comeback and swept the season series for the first time since 1935.

* Halas yelled at opposing players. He once shouted at Willie Davis "Hey #87 – Willie – your offsides." To which Lombardi responded "Get back in the box and leave my players alone!"7

Packers 7 21 3 0   31
Bears   7   0 7 14 28
Chi Ditka 47yd pass from Wade (LeClerc kick)
GB   Kramer 53yd pass from Starr (Hornung kick)
GB   Kramer 8yd pass from Starr (Hornung kick)
GB   Hornung 8yd run (Hornung kick)
GB   Hornung 34yd pass from Starr (Hornung kick)
GB   Hornung 51yd FG
Chi Ditka 15yd pass from Wade (LeClerc kick)
Chi Ditka 29yd pass from Wade (LeClerc kick)
Chi Casares 9yd run (LeClerc kick)

SEASON: Bears 8-6-0 (4th)   Packers 11-3-0 (1st)
                                Beat Giants 37-0
                                in title game

1962

9/30
Packers 49-0   City Stadium   38,669

Jim Taylor ran for three touchdowns and 126 yards as the Packers manhandled the Bears. Green Bay picked off five Chicago passes, and they held the Bears to 176 yards total yards. The Packers outgained the Bears 409 – 176.

* The Bears played without Bill George and Willie Galimore.

* This was the Packers' largest margin of victory in the rivalry. Lombardi was never comfortable with it.

Bears   0 0 0 0   0
Packers 0 14 21 14 49
GB Taylor 1yd run (Hornung kick)
GB Kramer 54yd pass from Starr (Hornung kick)
GB Taylor 3yd run (Hornung kick)
GB Pitts 26yd run (Hornung kick)
GB Taylor 11yd run (Hornung kick)
GB Starr 5yd run (Hornung kick)
GB Adderley 50yd interception return (Hornung kick)

....

11/4
Packers 38-7   Soldier Field   48,753

The Bears turned the ball over seven times. They gave Packer fullback Jim Taylor far too many chances, and he took the game away from them again. His four touchdowns and 124 yards made it another rout for Green Bay. They Packers outgained the Bears on the ground 215 – 65, and they improved their record to 8-0.

After two humiliating defeats in 1962, Halas and his coaches spent of the entire summer of 1963 game planning to defeat the Packers.

Packers 7 3 7 21 38
Bears   0 7 0 0   7
GB   Taylor 2 yard run (Kramer kick)
Chi Adams 4yd pass from Wade (LeClerc kick)
GB   Kramer 17yd FG
GB   Taylor 1yd run (Kramer kick)
GB   Taylor 1yd run (Kramer kick)
GB   Taylor 2yd run (Kramer kick)
GB   Gros 9yd run (Kramer kick)

SEASON: Bears 9-5-0 (3rd)   Packers 13-1-0 (1st)
*Beat Giants 16-7
in title game*

1963

9/15
Bears 10-3   **City Stadium**   **42,327**

The Bears wanted the defending champions. After the defeats of 1962, Chicago wanted revenge, and Halas was especially primed after hearing Lombardi speak confidently in the off-season about his team's chances for continued success against Chicago.

The Bears picked off Bart Starr four times and held the Packers to just nine first downs. Without Paul Hornung, who had been suspended indefinitely for gambling, Green Bay ran for just 77 yards and they never got closer than the Bears' 33. Jim Taylor's fumble led to the Bears' first points. In the third quarter, Rosey Taylor's interception was the turning point! It led to Billy Wade's 68 yard drive for the game's only touchdown. Wade led the Bears to the goal line with a series of short passes that kept Green Bay off balance. Marconi then took it across for the winner..

* Halas called this game "the greatest team effort in the history of the Chicago Bears."[8]

* This was the largest crowd to date to see a game in Green Bay.

Bears   3   0   7   0   10
Packers   3   0   0   0   3
Chi   Jencks 32yd FG
GB   Kramer 41yd FG
Chi   Marconi 1yd run (Jencks kick)

....

11/17
Bears 26-7   **Wrigley Field**   **49,166**

In the most highly anticipated game in Chicago Bear history, the Western Conference lead was at stake, and the Bears were still eager for more revenge! With Bart Starr out with a re-injured hand that he broke earlier in the season, the Bears dominated.

Chicago jumped in front on two Roger Leclerc field goals. Leclerc also recovered Herb Adderley's fumble that setup Willie Galimore's long touchdown run in the first quarter. In Starr's absence, John Roach and Zeke Bratkowski were a combined 11-30 with five interceptions. The running game also managed just 71 yards.

Meanwhile, the Bears blew through the Packers' defense for 248 yards on the ground. Seven Green Bay turnovers helped the Bears sweep the season series and give them a one game lead in the conference with four games to go.

The week of the game, Lombardi closed practices. A Bears practice was interrupted to investigate a photographer who was taking pictures from an apartment building overlooking Wrigley.

The game was blacked out within 75 miles of Chicago. A mass exodus of Bears fans headed for the suburbs.

Rick Casares suffered a broken leg from a hit by Ray Nitschke.

The Bears held the Packers to 10 points in two games. The team gave the game ball to their defensive assistant coach George Allen.

Packers 0 0 0 7   7
Bears   13 0 3 10 26
Chi LeClerc 29yd FG
Chi LeClerc 46yd FG
Chi Galimore 27yd run (Jencks kick)
Chi LeClerc 46yd FG
Chi LeClerc 46yd FG
Chi Wade 5yd run (Jencks kick)
GB Moore 11yd run (Kramer kick)

SEASON: Bears 11-1-2 (1st)   Packers 11-2-1 (2nd)
               Beat Giants 14-10
                 in title game

1964

9/13
Packers 23-12   City Stadium   42,327

This was the *Free Kick Game*, and it marked the triumphant return of Paul Hornung against the defending champion Bears! Hornung, who had been suspended for the entire 1963 season for gambling, picked up where he left off by scoring 11 of Green Bay's 23 points. Hornung kicked three field goals, including an unusual *free kick* field goal after a fair catch by Elijah Pitts at the Chicago 48 yard line. The kick, called by Lombardi, capitalized on a little-known rule that awards a free kick to the receiving team after a fair catch! Hornung made the free kick from 52 yards away, and the Packers went up 17-3 right before half.

Besides the "Golden Boy," Bart Starr threw two touchdown passes, and the Packers rolled over Chicago. Green Bay ran the ball for 197 yards (Chicago's 46), and the Bears' offense totaled 129 yards.

* During training camp, a tragic car accident took the lives of two young Chicago Bears - halfback Willie Galimore and receiver Bo Farrington.

Bears   0   3   9   0   12
Packers 7   10 3   3   23
GB   McGee 11yd pass from Starr (Hornung kick)
Chi Jencks 8yd FG
GB   Moore 33yd pass from Starr (Hornung kick)
GB   Hornung 52yd FG
Chi Jencks 36yd FG
Chi Ditka 13yd pass from Bukich (kick failed)
GB   Hornung 29yd FG
GB   Hornung 20yd FG

12/5
Packers 17-3   **Wrigley Field**   **43,636**

A two-day snowstorm that continued during the game dropped nearly a foot of snow on Chicago. The conditions didn't stop Willie Wood though who had a hand in all of Green Bay's 17 points. His punt returns of 64 and 42 yards setup both Packer touchdowns. In the fourth quarter, his interception led to a field goal.

Along the way, Chicago's quarterback Rudy Buchich was injured in the second quarter. He was replaced by Billy Wade. It didn't make much difference as Mike Ditka was also knocked out of the game by Ray Nitschke, and the Bears turned the ball over five times.

* *The night before the game Lombardi saw Paul Hornung with a date and sitting at bar in a Chicago restaurant. This was against Packer rules and Lombardi fined Hornung. Later, he reduced the fine when he learned that Hornung had not been drinking.*

* *Snowballs reigned down on the Packers the entire game.*

* *Taylor's 89 yards made him the first player in NFL history to rush for 1,000 yards five seasons in a row.*

* *Wrigley Field locker rooms left a lot to be desired especially when George Halas turned off the hot water!*

Packers 0 7 7 3   17
Bears   0 3 0 0   3
GB Hornung 5yd run (Hornung kick)
Chi LeClerc 31yd FG
GB Taylor 13yd run (Hornung kick)
GB Hornung 9yd FG

SEASON: Bears 5-9-0 (6th)   Packers 8-5-1 (2nd)

1965

10/3
Packers 23-14   **Lambeau Field**   **50,852**

The Packers renamed their stadium in honor of Curly Lambeau, who died suddenly of a heart attack at 67. An exciting contest followed with over 700 yards of offense!

Green Bay scored almost at will in the first half, and they led 20-0 at halftime. In the second half, quarterback Rudy Buckich and rookie halfback Gale Sayers sparked Chicago. Sayers scored two touchdowns in the second half including a spectacular 65 yard run after a short pass from Bukich. He electrified the Packer crowd and gave anyone who saw the run an early glimpse of his greatness.

The Bears eventually closed to within nine, but Green Bay's three touchdown in the first half proved too much to overcome.

* A tough loss for the Bears. They had a touchdown called back, and they outgained the Packers (413-299).

* This was Gale Sayers' first start. He finished the game with 80 yards on 17 carries. Prior to this game, many fans questioned his ability and toughness.

Bears   0   0   7   7   14
Packers 14   6   3   0   23
GB   Hornung 1yd run (Chandler kick)
GB   Caffey 42yd interception return (Chandler kick)
GB   Long 48yd pass from Starr (kick blocked)
GB   Chandler 16yd FG
Chi   Sayers 6yd run (LeClerc kick)
Chi   Sayers 65yd pass from Bukich (LeClerc kick)

10/31
Bears 31-10   **Wrigley Field**   **45,664**

The undefeated Packers (6-0) visit Wrigley Field on Halloween. They scored first, but defensive pressure on Starr forced two Interceptions that put the Bears in control. Doug Atkins and Bennie McRae made the steals, and the Bears' running game took it from there. Gale Sayers' 66 yard punt return set up the touchdown that put the game out of reach. The Bears kept the ball away from the Packers with 212 yards rushing.

Lombardi after the game: "This Bear team is better than the 1963 bunch that won the championship."[9]

Packers 7 3 0   0 10
Bears   0 17 7 7 31
GB   Taylor 1yd run (Chandler kick)
Chi LeClerc 24yd FG
Chi Jones 13yd pass from Bukich (LeClerc kick)
Chi Sayers 10yd run (LeClerc kick)
GB   Chandler 43yd FG
Chi Arnett 2yd run (LeClerc kick)
Chi Bull 4yd run (LeClerc kick)

Season: Bears 9-5-0 (3rd)   Packers 10-3-1 (1st)
                              *Beat Browns 23-12
                              in title game*

1966

10/16
Packers 17-0   **Wrigley Field**   **50,852**

A scoreless first half finally gave way to a third quarter touchdown by Green Bay. On Green Bay's 66 yard scoring drive, Jim Taylor picked up 39 yards before Paul Hornung scored from the one. Ray Nitschke's interception then led to a field goal. Finally, Willie Wood returned another Buchich pass 20 yards for a touchdown. A dominant Green Bay defense held Gale Sayers to 29 yards. The Bears gained just 94 yards with six first downs.

* *This is the first time since the rivals began playing more than one game that the first game was played in Chicago.*

* *When the Packers practiced in Wrigley, they wore different numbers to confuse the alleged spies in the apartment buildings across the street.*

* *On Paul Hornung's touchdown, he suffered a neck injury on a hit by Doug Buffone, that would eventually end his career.*

Packers   0   0   10   7   17
Bears   0   0   0   0
GB   Hornung 1yd run (Chandler kick)
GB   Chandler 30yd FG
GB   Wood 20yd pass interception return (Chandler kick

....

11/20
Packers 13-6   Lambeau Field   50,861

Even though quarterback Bart Starr was hurt on the second play and had to leave the game, his backup Zeke Bratkowski saved the day. Though Green Bay had difficulty running the ball, Bratkowski, a former Bear, had a fine day passing with 187 yards and two touchdowns.

Down 7-0 in the fourth, Gale Sayers scored for the Bears with just under ten minutes left. Roger LeClerc missed the extra point that would have tied the game. On the ensuing drive, the Packers went 63 yards to clinch it with a secomd Carroll Dale touchdown.

* *Eighteen penalties were called for 178 yards!*

Bears   0 0 0 6   6
Packers 0 7 0 6 13
GB Dale 6yd pass from Bratkowski (Chandler kick)
Chi Sayers 2yd run (kick failed)
GB Dale 33 yd pass from Bratkowski (kick failed)

SEASON: Bears 5-7-2 (5th)   Packers 12-2-0 (1st)
*Beat Chiefs 35-10
in Super Bowl I*

1967

9/24
Packers 13-10   Lambeau Field   50,861

Bart Starr threw five interceptions. Richie Pettibon stole three of them. The Packers fumbled three times. Dick Butkus recovered two of them. Green Bay still won! The Packers outgained the Bears by more than 200 yards, yet Gale Sayers tied it with a late fourth quarter touchdown. In a classic two-minute drill by the venerable Starr, Green Bay drove into field position for Don Candler's winning kick with 1:03 left.

Bears   0 0 3 7 10
Packers 0 10 0 3 13
GB Grabowski 2yd run (Chandler kick)
GB Chandler 20yd FG
Chi Percival 22yd FG
Chi Sayers 13yd run (Percival kick)
GB Chandler 46yd FG

11/26
Packers 17-13   Wrigley Field   47,513

As head coaches, this was the last game between Halas and Lombardi. Both men moved into front office positions following the season.

An interception by linebacker Dave Robinson setup a Bart Starr to Boyd Dowler touchdown pass that gave Green Bay an early lead. It was one of six catches by Dowler on the afternoon for over 100 yards. The Bears then tied the game on a spectacular touchdown run by Gale Sayers.

Leading 14-10 at halftime, the Packers recovered a Sayers fumble and convert with a field goal for some breathing room. Sayers ran for more yards than the entire Packer team. The Bears passed for just 23 yards and they turned the ball over three times.

* *The win gives Green Bay the chance to play for their third straight championship.*

* *Twenty-five hundred fans greeted the Packers at Austin Straubel Field in Green Bay.*

* *Halas' record against the Packers > 42-30-4 / Against Lombardi > 13-5*

Packers 7   7   3   0   17
Bears   7   3   0   3   13
GB   Dowler 5yd pass from Starr (Chandler kick)
Chi Sayers 43yd run (Percival kick)
GB   Anderson 1yd run (Chandler kick)
Chi Percival 10yd FG
GB   Chandler 38yd FG
Chi Percival 15yd FG

SEASON: Bears 7-6-1 (2nd)   Packers 9-4-1 (1st)
Beat Raiders 33-14
in Super Bowl II

1968

11/3
Bears 13-10 Lambeau Field 50,861

George Halas and Vince Lombardi were replaced by loyal assistant coaches: Jim Dooley of the Bears and Phil Bengston of the Packers. In their first meeting, a low scoring, defensive battle pitted the great Gale Sayers against an aging Packer defense.

Sayers won the battle with the greatest game of his career. He ran and spun his way through Green Bay defense all afternoon for 205 yards!! But he was not the hero That honor went to Matt Percival, who kicked two field goals, including the unusual game winner with less than a minute to play. When Chicago's Cecil Turner called for a fair catch of a Donny Anderson punt at the Green Bay 46 yard line, a *free kick* was awarded to Chicago "after one team makes a fair catch of a punt."[10] The kick was reminiscent of Paul Hornung's successful *free kick* against the Bears just before the halftime in 1964. But Percival's kick was for all the marbles and a bit more special than Hornung's.

* Poor kicking plagued the Packers all season. In this game, they missed three field goals from 22, 27 and 44 yards.

Bears   0 3 7 3   13
Packers 0 0 7 3   10
Chi Percival 10yd FG
Chi Carter 2yd run (Percival kick)
GB   Dale 50yd pass from Starr (Mercein kick)
GB   Mercein 19yd FG
Chi Percival 43yd FG

12/15
Packers 28-27   **Wrigley Field**   **46,435**

The Packers were out of the playoff picture, and they hoped to play the spoiler in this game. With Bart Starr injured, and backup Zeke Bratkowski hurt in the first quarter, Don Horn, who had been activated earlier in the day, led Green Bay.

Four fantastic touchdown passes of more than 48 yards were thrown in this game – two by Jack Concannon of the Bears and one each by Bratkowski and Horn. But it was Horn's short scoring pass to Boyd Dowler in the third quarter that provided the margin of victory. The Bears stormed back from a 28-10 deficit in the third quarter to make it a game. But with 1:13 left to play, Ray Nitschke's interception preserved the win for Green Bay. The loss knocked the Bears out of the playoffs and gave the Central Divison title to the Minnesota Vikings.

Dick Butkus baited and intimidated the young Don Horn calling him "Tin Horn" and "Green Horn."

When George Seals of the Bears was hurt, Ray Nitschke stood over Seals and taunted him. The Bears, needless to say, were not pleased.

Packers 7 14 7   0 28
Bears   10   0 0 17 27
Chi Percival 14yd FG
GB   Dowler 72yd pass from Bratkowski (Mercer kick)
Chi Gordon 48yd pass from Jack Concannon (Percival kick)
GB   Grabowski 67yd pass from Horn (Mercer kick)
GB   Mercein 1yd run (Mercer kick)
GB   Dowler 25yd pass from Horn (Mercer kick)
Chi Bull 8yd run (Percival kick)
Chi Percival 26yd FG
Chi Gordon 51yd pass from Concannon (Percival kick)

SEASON: Bears 7-7-0 (2nd)   Packers 6-7-1 (3rd)

1969

9/21
Packers 17-0 **Lambeau Field** **50,861**

The 100th meeting between the Bears and Packers belonged to Travis Williams. He outgained Gale Sayers 67-31, and he also caught a touchdown pass from Bart Starr.

The Packers dominated with a stingy defense and a strong running attack. They held Chicago to 12 first downs and 90 yards on the ground. Green Bay ran for 196 yards! Chicago never got inside the Packers' 30 yard line, and two interceptions by Doug Hart helped keep the Bears off the scoreboard.

Bears   0   0   0   0   0
Packers 7   0   0   10   17
GB   Williams 31yd pass from Starr (Mercer kick)
GB   Grabowski 1yd run (Mercer kick)
GB   Mercer 32yd FG

....

12/14
Packers 21-3 **Wrigley Field** **45,216**

This was a scoreless game at halftime thanks to Booth Lusteg's three missed three field goals for Green Bay. The Packers exploded for 21 points in the third quarter. Travis Williams blew through the Chicago defense with a long touchdown run and, later in the quarter, he caught a 60 yard touchdown pass from Don Horn. The Packers held Chicago's passing game in check (62 yards) while also throwing for 190 yards themselves.

After a first half in which he went 2 for 17 in passing, Chicago quarterback Virgil Carter blasted the Bears in the media for taking him out of the game. He was fined $1,000 by Halas and never played for the Bears again.

Packers 0 0 21 0 21
Bears   0 0   0 3   3
GB Williams 39yd run (Lusteg kick)
GB Fleming 10yd pass from Horn (Lusteg kick)
GB Williams 60yd pass from Horn (Lusteg kick)
Chi Percival 34yd FG

SEASON: Bears 1-13-0 (4th)   Packers 8-6-0 (3rd)

Rivalry Stars of the 1960s

Mike Ditka   1961-66, 192-92   TE, Coach
The competitive fire of Mike Ditka stoked three decades of the rivalry game. He was a new breed of tight end who could catch as well as block. He burst on the scene in '61, leading all tight ends with 58 catches, and he was named Rookie of the Year. Ditka was the first tight end elected to the Hall of Fame. He was a captain of the 1963 championship team and, after retiring as a player he returned to lead the Bears back to the top as head coach in 1982.

Dick Butkus   1965-73   MLB
Chicago native Dick Butkus graduated from Illinois. He was the third pick in the 1965 draft, just ahead of Gale Sayers. As the Bears' intimidating middle linebacker, his vicious hits and ability to rip the ball from opponent were frightening. His never ending effort and pursuits are legendary. In his nine-year career, Butkus was a first team All-Pro six times, and he is rated as one of the top ten players of all-time in many rankings.

Gale Sayers   1965-71   HB
A graduate of Kansas, Sayers was the most naturally gifted running back of his generation. A brilliant athlete, Sayers could run, cut, jump and fake with unmatched fluidity and grace. He led the league in rushing twice (1966, 1969) and was arguably the most-feared halfback

in the league during his injury riddled seven-year career. His knee injuries, which began near the end of the 1968 season, eventually brought his career to an end.

⭐

Bart Starr   1956-71, 1975-83   QB, Coach

Starr graduated from Alabama in 1956, and he was drafted in the 17th round by Green Bay. Starr was an outstanding leader who rarely made a mistake with the football. He led the Packers to five championships, and he was the league's MVP in 1966 and the MVP of the first two Super Bowls. Starr returned to Green Bay to coach the Packers, but he did not have as much success as a coach as he had as a player.

Ray Nitschke   1958-72   MLB

Ray Nitschke was an All-American at Illinois who played his entire career in Green Bay (1958-1972). He began to live-up to his potential once he got married, and Vince Lombardi became his head coach. He became a starter in 1962 and was the MVP of the 1962 NFL Championship Game. Nitschke went on to become the heart and soul of the Packers' defense. He was tough, intimidating and a vicious hitter. His #66 is one of five numbers retired by Green Bay.

Vince Lombardi   1959-68   Coach

The Packers hired Lombardi away from the New York Giants in 1959. In his second year, Green Bay was in the NFL Championship Game. Lombardi turned the Packers around and won five championships in seven years. That dominance has never been equaled. One of the greatest coaches of all time, Lombardi's career record was 90-30-4 (.766). He had a warm relationship with Halas, even though he had a winning record against him (13-5).

The Games

1970-79
Wins
Bears 11 　　　　　 Packers 9
Series: 65-50-6 Bears

Changes abound in the NFL in the seventies. While football had already passed baseball as the country'as most-popular sport, the nine new teams from the American Football League brought a new excitement to the league. Seattle and Tampa Bay also began play in 1976. New divisions, new conferences and new rivalries won over millions of more fans. Super Bowl Sunday was well on its way to becoming an American institution.

In 1970, Monday Night Football attracted whole new audience of fans. The entertaining banter between Howard Cosell, Frank Gifford and Don Merideth made the broadcast a popular staple in living rooms and entertainment venues nationwide. The NFL was a ratings winner with more sponsors and prime time opportunities waiting just around the corner. In 1978, the league accommodated the interest by adding two more games to the schedule making it 16 game season.

In 1978, three rule changes profoundly changed the game. The changes encouraged more passing which became the name of the game in the 1980s.

* Offensive lineman could now extend their arms, open their hands, and grab inside of the opponent's shoulders pads
* Defensive backs could no longer make contact with receivers after the first five yards
* Deflected balls were now *in play* which created new scoring possibilities with tip drills and other creative plays

For the Bears and the Packers, the 1970s were a lean decade.

Each franchise had just two winning seasons. The Bears made the playoffs twice, and the Packers once. Neither won a championship. Chicago tried four head coaches in nine years, and the Packers reached back to Bart Starr to lead them out of the post-Lombardi wilderness. Nothing worked for either team.

1970

11/15
Packers 20-19   Lambeau Field   56,263

Quarterback Bart Starr, playing his first full game in a month, led a thrilling Green Bay comeback. After Green Bay led at the halftime 10-0, Jack Concannon's arm and Matt Percival's toe led the Chicago back.

At the start of the fourth quarter, they had narrowed the lead to 13-10. Thanks to Percival's toe, they went in front 19-13. Then with 1:10 left in the game, Bart Starr began a legendary drive for the Packers. Along the way, he connected with four different receivers as he marched the Packers 77 yards to the Chicago three yard line. With three seconds left and his receivers covered, Starr scrambled around right end for the winning score!

Bears   0   0   10   9   19
Packers 10   0   3   7   20
GB Livingston 17yd FG
GB Anderson 17yd run (Livingston kick)
Chi Percival 23yd FG
Chi Gordon 79yd pass from Concannon (Percival kick)
GB Livingston 49yd FG
Chi Percival 38yd FG
Chi Percival 13yd FG
Chi Percival 31yd FG
GB Starr 3yd run (Livingston kick)

12/13
Bears 35-17   **Wrigley Field**   **44,957**

This is the last Bear-Packer game at Wrigley Field, and the Bears use it snap their four game losing streak to Green Bay. Quarterback Jack Concannon led the way for Chicago with 338 yards passing, four touchdown passes and one touchdown run!

For Green Bay, Dick Butkus and Willie Holman sacked Bart Starr in the first quarter. Starr came up wobbly, and he left the field briefly. He returned to throw one pass to Carroll Dale before sitting down on the field disoriented. Starr left the game, and he took the offense with him. The Bears sacked his replacement, rookie Frank Patrick, six times.

Passing Yards: Chicago 341 Green Bay 161

Packers 3 0 0 14   17
Bears   14 7 7 7   35
Chi Gordon 15yd pass from Concannon (Percival kick)
Chi Farmer 42yd pass from Concannon (Percival kick)
GB   Livingston 32yd FG
Chi Concannon 15yd run (Percival kick)
Chi Gordon 25yd pass from Concannon (Percival kick)
GB   Anderson 7yd run (Livingston kick)
Chi Ogden 6yd pass from Concannon (Percival kick)
GB   Hilton 29yd pass from Norton (Livingston kick)

SEASON: Bears 6-8-0 (3rd)   Packers 6-8-0 (3rd)

1971

11/7
Packers 17-14   **Soldier Field**   **55,049**

This is the first Bear-Packer game at Soldier Field since 1926! Green Bay dominated the first half with fullback John Brockington. Brockington scored one touchdown and gained 142 yards on the afternoon. Bears' quarterback Bobby Douglass didn't help matters with three interceptions. He also didn't get the ball inside Green Bay's 30 yard line until the fourth quarter.

In the fourth quarter, after the Dick Butkus recovered a fumble that led to the tying touchdown, Dave Hampton returned the ensuing kickoff 62 yards for Green Bay! It setup a Lou Michaels field goal with 59 seconds left for the win.

Packers   0   14   0   3   17
Bears   0   0   0   14   14
GB   Dale 31yd pass from Hunter (Michaels kick)
GB   Brockington 7yd run (Michaels kick)
Chi Farmer 30yd pass from Douglass (Percival kick)
Chi Douglass 1yd run (Percival kick)
GB   Michaels 22yd

12/12
Packers 31-10   **Lambeau Field**   **56,263**

The Packers swept the season series on Ray Nitschke Day! They jumped in front on a Scott Hunter bomb to Carroll Dale on their first possession. Chicago stayed close until the second half, but they could not keep up. Touchdowns by Brockington, Hunter and Starr, put the game away.

This was Bart Starr's last game against the Bears as a player.

Bears   7   0   3   0   10
Packers   7   0   14   10   31
GB   Dale 77 yd pass from Hunter (Webster kick)
Chi Gordon 31yd pass from Nix (Percival kick)
GB   Brockington 6yd run (Webster kick)
GB   Hunter 1yd run (Webster kick)
Chi Percival 12yd FG
GB   Starr 1yd run (Webster kick)
GB   Webster 27 yd FG

SEASON: Bears 6-8-0 (3rd)   Packers 4-8-2 (4th)

1972

10/8
Packers 20-17   Lambeau Field   56,263

A fumble recovery got the Packers off to a fast start. Just before halftime, they extended their lead on a 48 yard pass that was deflected into the arms of receiver Jon Staggers for a touchdown.

The Bears came back in the second half. Quarterback Bobby Douglas led two drives for touchdowns, one of which he scored with nine minutes left to tie the game. Scott Hunter then drove Green Bay downfield for a field goal by rookie Chester Marcol with 30 seconds to go. With five seconds remaining, Mac Percival's 51 yarder to tie the game for the Bears fell short.

* *This was Abe Gibron's first game as coach against the Packers.*

Bears   0   3   7   7   17
Packers   7 10   0   3   20
GB   Williams 21yd fumble recovery return (Marcol kick)
Chi   Percival 12yd FG
GB   Staggers 48yd pass from Hunter (Marcol kick)
GB   Marcol 26yd FG
Chi   Pinder 2yd run (Percival kick)
Chi   Douglass 1yd run (Percival kick)
GB   Marcol 37yd FG

....

11/12
Packers 23-17   Soldier Field   55,701

Chester Marcol beats the Bears again. This time, he kicked three field goals, and the Packers won despite not completing a pass in the first half. Marcol was also a marked man. Chicago coach Abe Gibron sent in Gary Kosins to *take out* Marcol after a kickoff, but he wasn't successful. Dick Butkus instead knocked Packer quarterback Scott Hunter out of the game in the first half. Jerry Tagge then made his Packer debut, and he completed four of seven passes.

Green Bay won despite just eight first downs and 163 yards. The Bears won the statistical battle, but Marcol had the final word.

Gary Kosins, who was sent in to get Marcol, was from Milwaukee and his family name was Kosinski. In 1973, Gibron would call Marcol the Polish Prince!

Packers 14 3 3 3 23
Bears   7 0 3 7 17
GB Brockington 12yd run (Marcol kick)
Chi Pinder 4yd run (Percival kick)
GB Hunter 1yd run (Marcol kick)
GB Marcol 51 yd FG
Chi Percival 38yd FG
GB Marcol 21yd FG
Chi Douglass 1yd run (Percival kick)
GB Marcol 21yd FG

SEASON: Bears 4-9-1 (4th)   Packers 10-4-0 (1st)

1973

11/4
Bears 31-17   **Lambeau Field**   **53,231**

This was Bobby Douglas' greatest game as the quarterback of the Chicago Bears. He ran for 100 yards, scored four touchdowns and threw for 118 yards on 10 for 15 passing. His play making ability led a great second half comeback for the Bears.

Chicago's defense was dominant. They held Green Bay to just 98 total yards and eight first downs (one in the second half). They passed for -12 yards, and the Bears sacked Packer quarterback Scott Hunter four times.

Green Bay did not gain over 100 yards for the third time this season.

Bears   7 3 14 7 31
Packers 7 10 0 0 17
Chi Douglass 1yd run (Percival kick)
GB Lane 5yd pass from Hunter (Marcol kick)
GB Hunter 1yd run (Marcol kick)
GB Marcol 25yd FG
Chi Percival 10yd FG
Chi Douglass 1yd run (Percival kick)
Chi Douglass 2yd run (Percival kick)
Chi Douglass 1yd run (Percival kick)

....

12/16
Packers 21-0   **Soldier Field**   **29,157**

An inch of ice greeted the fans. Both teams closed out dismal seasons with the Bears (3-11) last in the Central Division and Green Bay just a notch above (5-7-2).

The Packers dominated on the ground. Most of their 298 yards were picked up by their big backfiekd of John Brockington (142 yards) and McArthur Lane (101 yards). Brockington's 53 yard run set up the first and only touchdown Green Bay would need. The Packers completed just three passes all game, but two went for touchdowns. They also pressured Chicago quarterback Gary Huff all afternoon and sacked him six times.

There were 26,544 no shows.

Packers 7 7 0 7 21
Bears   0 0 0 0 0
GB Staggers 20yd pass from Tagge (Marcol kick)
GB Goodman 3yd run (Marcol kick)
GB Staggers 36yd pass from Tagge (Marcol kick)

SEASON: Bears 3-11-0 (4th)   Packers 5-7-2 (3rd)

1974

10/21
Bears 10-9 **Soldier Field** **50,623**

It's Monday Night Football! The Bears went up early and held on as the Packers crept back into the game in the second half. Fortunately for Chicago, Green Bay got back in the game only behind the toe of Chester Marcol. Marcol accounted for all of Green Bay's points with three field goals. A Ted Hendricks interception return of 44 yards setup one of the kicks. Green Bay's offense failed to produce more despite recovering three Chicago fumbles inside the Bears' 37 yard line.

* Two days after this loss, the Packers traded five draft choices to the Los Angeles Rams for quarterback John Hadl.

Packers 0 0 6 3   9
Bears   10 0 0 0 10
Chi Roder 23yd FG
Chi Wade 57yd pass from Gary Huff (Roder kick)
GB   Marcol 3yd FG
GB   Marcol 33yd FG
GB   Marcol 36yd FG

....

11/10
Packers 20-3 **County Stadium** **46,567**

The Packers began playing games in Milwaukee in 1933. This was the only game that they played there against the Bears. A steady rain made it so sloppy that the Chicago Tribune reported that play was like "one of those electric football games gone haywire."[11] Rookie Steve Odom's 95 yard punt return just before halftime gave the Packers the lead that they never relinquished. Their defense did the job all day with four sacks, four fumble recoveries and an interception.

* Odom's return was a Green Bay record. It broke Veryl Switzer's 93 yard return in 1954 also against the Bears.

```
Bears      3   0   0   0    3
Packers    0  10   0  10   20
```
Chi Roder 44yd FG
GB   Marcol 45yd FG
GB   Odom 95yd punt return (Marcol kick)
GB   Marcol 24yd FG
GB   Brockington 1yd run (Marcol kick)

SEASON: Bears 4-10-0 (4th)   Packers 6-8-0 (3rd)

1975

11/9
Bears 27-14   **Soldier Field**   **48,738**

This was Walter Payton's first game against Green Bay. Though he gained just 49 yards on 14 carries, his touchdown pushed Chicago's lead to 17-7 before halftime. In the third period, Green Bay's back-up quarterback Don Milan (in place of John Hadl), threw an interception to Craig Clemens, who streaked 76 yards down the sideline for a touchdown to put the game out of reach. The Bears' defense held Green Bay to just 41 yards on the ground.

* Both teams had new coaches: Bart Starr and Jack Pardee.

```
Packers   0   7   0   7   14
Bears    10   7  10   0   27
```
Chi Thomas 34yd FG
Chi Parsons 12yd pass from Gary Huff (Thomas kick)
GB   Odom, 42-yard pass from Milan (Danelo kick)
Chi Payton 5yd run (Thomas kick)
Chi Thomas 48yd FG
Chi Clemons, 76-yard interception return (Thomas kick)
GB   Smith 18yd pass from Brown (Danelo kick)

11/30
Packers 28-7   **Lambeau Field**   46,821

A steady snowfall and below zero wind chills made it a slippery game of 10 fumbles. Green Bay defensive tackle Dave Purifoy was involved with two of the fumbles, both resulting in Packer touchdowns. John Brockington ran for 111 yards and three touchdowns to overwhelm Chicago. The Packers' defense dominated, giving up just 132 yards, and Bears' quarterback Bob Avellini didn't complete a pass until Green Bay was in front 21-0.

* There were 29,000 no shows!

* The Chicago Tribune called this game the Cellar Bowl. Fans booed each team as they both finished 4-10 in 1975.

Bears   0   7   0   0   7
Packers   7 21   0   0   28
GB Brockington 1yd run (Danelo kick)
GB Brockington 1yd run (Danelo kick)
GB Odom 14yd pass from Harrell (Danelo kick)
GB Brockington 8yd run (Danelo kick)
Chi Payton 1yd run (Thomas kick)

SEASON: Bears 4-10-0 (3rd)   Packers 4-10-0 (3rd)

1976

11/14
Bears 24-13   **Soldier Field**   52,907

In the first quarter, the Bears converted two Green Bay fumbles into touchdowns. Walter Payton scored the first one and he ran for 109 yards on the day. After the Packers trimmed the lead to 14-13 in the second half, Roland Harper ripped off a 16 yard touchdown run for the winning points. Four costly turnovers and quarterback Lynn

Dickey's bruised shoulder prevented any Green Bay comeback.

* Eighteen penalties were called for 150 yards. After the game, Dave Roller of the Packers took exception to several cheap shots he thought the Bears had taken at Lynn Dickey.

Packers   0   10   3   0   13
Bears   14   0   7   3   24
Chi Payton 2yd run (Thomas kick)
Chi Adamle 4yd pass from Avellini (Thomas kick)
GB   Payne 27yd pass from Dickey (Marcol kick)
GB   Marcol 19yd FG
GB   Marcol 27yd FG
Chi Harper 16yd run (Thomas kick)
Chi Thomas 46yd FG

....

11/28
Bears 16-10   Lambeau Field   56,267

Two weeks later, Walter Payton ran for 110 yards and the Bears swept the season series for the first time since 1963. They prevailed in wind chills as low as -14 degrees which was, to that point, the second coldest game in Packer history. Turnstiles froze. Band instruments froze. The Packer offense froze! Green Bay turned the ball over four times and they picked up just 11 first downs. Though the Packers tied it early in the third quarter, Bob Thomas' two field goals won it.

* Before the game, Dave Roller claimed he would "get" Bob Avellini.

Bears   10   0   3   3   16
Packers   0   3   7   0   10
Chi Bob Thomas 40yd FG
Chi Scott 49yd pass from Avellini (Thomas kick)
GB   Marcol 45yd FG
GB   Payne 11yd pass from Brown (Marcol kick)
Chi Thomas 22yd FG
Chi Thomas 25yd FG

SEASON: Bears 7-7-0 (2nd)   Packers 5-9-0 (4th)

1977

10/30
Bears 26-0**Lambeau Field****56,002**

The last time the Bears shut out the Packers was 1949! The Packers were so inept in the first half that their fans booed at halftime.

Walter Payton led Chicago's ground attack with 117 yards at the end of the first quarter alone. The Packer defense was pounded by a ground game that ran 54 times for for 375 yards. Payton tied Gale Sayers' single game rushing record of 205 yards. Ironically, Sayers set the record against the Packers in 1968. "Sweetness" scored two touchdowns, and he came out of the game with 11 minutes still remaining.

Total Yards: Bears 419 Packers 197

Bears   13   3   0   10   26
Packers   0   0   0   0   0
Chi Musso 3yd run (run failed)
Chi Payton 6yd run (Thomas kick)
Chi Thomas 47yd FG
Chi Payton 1yd run (Thomas kick)
Chi Thomas 20yd FG

....

12/11
Bears 21-10**Soldier Field****33,557**

This is the Bears' fourth consecutive win over Green Bay. It's also Walter Payton's fourth straight 100 yard game against the Packers. In below zero temperatures, Payton ran for 163 yards and two touchdowns. Chicago led 14-10 at halftime, and they held the Packers scoreless in the second half while adding to their lead.

Packers   0   10   0   0   10
Bears   7   7   0   7   21
Chi Scott 11yd pass from Avellini Thomas kick)
GB   Marcol 19yd FG

Chi Payton 1yd run (Thomas kick)
GB   Smith 7yd run (Marcol kick)
Chi Payton 7yd run (Thomas kick)

SEASON: Bears 9-5-0 (2nd)   Packers 4-10-0 (4th)

1978
10/8
Packers 24-14   Lambeau Field   55,352

This is Neil Armstrong's first rivalry game as head coach of the Chicago Bears. Green Bay's safety Steve Luke spoiled it. Luke recovered a Walter Payton fumble and the Packers took a 3-0 lead. In the third quarter, Luke also intercepted a deflected Bob Avellini pass and returned it 63 yards for a touchdown. The pick-six put the Packers up 17-0. Green Bay's defense forced five turnovers, negating the Bears overall advantage in yards gained (357-166).

Before the game, Payton questioned the legitimacy of Green Bay's fast start in 1978. It became bulletin board material. Payton was held to 82 yards.

Bears   0 0 0 14 14
Packers 0 3 14 7 24
GB   Marcol 41yd FG
GB   Middleton 2yd run (Marcol kick)
GB   Luke 63yd interception return (Marcol kick)
Chi Scott 15yd pass from Avellini (Thomas kick)
GB   Lofton 58yd pass from Whitehurst (Marcol kick)
Chi Scott 17yd pass from Avellini (Thomas kick)

....

12/10
Bears 14-0   Soldier Field   34,306

The Bears fought -10 degree wind chills to take advantage of two Packer turnovers and keep Green Bay out of the playoffs. Before halftime, Doug Plank of the Bears stripped the ball from Terdell Middleton. The fumble recovery began an 80 yard Chicago drive that ended with Walter Payton's touchdown. In the third quarter, Johnny Gray fumbled a punt, and the Bears scored a few plays later putting the game beyond the reach of Green Bay's weak offense that produced just 161 yards.

With an ineffective offense all afternoon, Bobby Douglas finished the game at quarterback for Green Bay!

```
Packers  0  0  0   0    0
Bears    0  7  7   0   14
```
Chi Payton 1yd run (Thomas kick)
Chi Scott 35yd pass from Phipps (Thomas kick)

SEASON: Bears 7-9-0 (4th)   Packers 8-7-1 (2nd)

1979
9/2
Bears 6-3   Soldier Field   56,515

A warm day greeted the unveiling of renovated Soldier Field. To christen the renovation, the Bears' defense reeked havoc on Green Bay quarterback David Whitehurst all afternoon. They sacked him six times and held the Packer offense to 149 total yards.

Walter Payton carried the ball 36 times for 125 yards. Along with Bob Thomas' two fields, that's all Chicago would need. Chester Marcol's attempt to tie the game late in the third quarter was blocked by Virgil Livers.

On his third carry, Packer rookie Eddie Lee Ivery injured his knee and was lost for the year. Two years later, Ivery again critically injured his knee at Soldier Field.

Packers 0 0 3 0   3
Bears   0 6 0 0   6
Chi Thomas 25yd FG
Chi Thomas 19yd FG
GB   Marcol 28yd FG

....

12/9
Bears 15-14   Lambeau Field   54,207

Though the Packers turned the ball over five times and ran for just 55 yards, they clung to a 7-6 lead in the fourth quarter. Tom Hicks of the Bears then picked off a Lynn Dickey screen pass and returned it 66 yards to put Chicago in control. When Green Bay fumbled the ensuing kickoff at their 31 yard line, Bob Thomas hit his third field goal of the day to provide the winning margin. Paul Coffman's second touchdown closed it to 15-14, but Tom Birney's 52 yard field goal try with 32 seconds left fell short.

Green Bay started slowly with nine penalties in the first half. There were sixteen penalties in the game for 133 yards (GB 10-64, Chi 6-69).

Bears   3 3 0 9   15
Packers 0 7 0 7   14
Chi Thomas 34yd FG
GB   Coffman 6yd pass from Dickey (Birney kick)
Chi Thomas 33yd FG
Chi Hicks 66yd interception return (kick failed)
Chi Thomas 44yd FG
GB   Coffman 22yd pass from Dickey (Birney kick)

SEASON: Bears 10-6-0 (2nd)   Packers 5-11-0 (4th)

Rivalry Stars of the 1970s

The seventies was a forgettable decade for both franchises. The rivalry became more about staying out of last place than winning championships.

1970-79	W	L	Pct.	Last Place	Next to Last
Bears	60	81	.425	'72, '73, '74	'70, '71, '75, '78
Packers	57	83	.404	'70, '71, '75 '76	'73, '74, '77, '79

Doug Buffone   1966-79   LB

When Doug Buffone retired in 1979, he had played in more games as a Chicago Bear than any other player. He was also the last player to have played for the Bears' founder George "Papa Bear" Halas. A fourth round pick out of Louisville, Buffone was the Bears defensive captain beginning in 1972. He still holds the franchise record for sacks in a single season (18) and for the most career interceptions by a linebacker (28).

Bobby Douglass   1969-77   QB

A second round draft choice out of Kansas in 1969, Douglass was the finest running quarterback in Chicago Bear history. In 1972, his 968 yards on the ground were the most ever by an NFL quarterback. The record stood for 34 years. Douglass was the Bears starting quarterback for four seasons, and he was a back-up for the Packers before retiring in 1978.

☆

John Brockington   1971-77   RB

From Ohio State, Brockington was the Packers' first round draft choice in 1971. He arrived as advertised – strong and fast. He was the Offensive Rookie of the Year in 1971, and he became the first running back in NFL history to top 1,000 yards in each of his first three seasons! Brockington teamed with McArthur Lane to give the Packers one of the league's top backfield's from 1972-74.

Larry "Rock" McCarren   1973-84   C

A native of Park Forest, Illinois, McCarren graduated from Illinois in 1973. He anchored Green Bay's offensive line for eleven years, and he played in 162 consecutive games. After retiring as a player, McCarren has been involved in broadcasting, and since 1995, he has been part of the Packer Radio Network.

The Games
1980-89
Wins

Bears 11   Packers 7

Series: 76-57-6 Bears

The NFL is a booming, big business in its seventh decade. New radio and television contracts generated plenty of revenue, and the league easily fended off its latest challenge from the United States Football League (USFL).

Three franchises relocated in the eighties. The Oakland Raiders moved to Los Angeles in 1982, and the Baltimore Colts left Maryland *at midnight* for Indianapolis in 1984. At the end of the decade, the St. Louis Cardinals relocated to Phoenix, Arizona.

Two strikes by the players interrupted play for 57 days in 1982 and 24 days in 1987. It didn't deter the fans. When play resumed after both strikes, attendance continued to soar. Games were more exciting than ever as the 1978 rule changes that encouraged more passing sure seemed to be working as "...footballs began flying like mad.....more passes were thrown per game, for more yards, than at any time in history."[12] To keep a closer eye on all of the action, *instant replay* was launched in 1986. The league began to seriously market itself in Europe with a preseason game - *The American Bowl*. In 1989, the new commissione promised to expand this effort and bring a regular season game overseas.

In the rivalry game, the eighties belonged to the Bears. With a new coach and excellent draft choices, the Bears rode the Super Bowl Shuffle all the way to the championsjip in 1985! During the Ditka-Gregg Era, games became ugly slugfests. Dirty play was common, and both Hall of Fame coaches showed little regard for policing the actions of their players. The Packers didn't win a game against Chicago for five years (1984-88), but when they did, it was one of the rivalry's most controversial. To this day, the "Instant Replay Game" is an anathema to every Bears fan that remembers it.

Overall, the Packers continued to stumble in the eighties. Two former players – Bart Starr and Forrest Gregg – failed as coaches and the franchise reacquired the *Siberia* reputation that was reminiscent of the fifties. Relief arrived in 1992 with a new general manager, a new coach and a new quarterback.

1980

9/7
Packers 12-6 (OT)   Lambeau Field   54,381

The 1980s began with the rivalry's most-bizarre ending. In a game where Walter Payton ran for just 65 yards, inept offenses and field goals ruled the afternoon. In the overtime period, Chester Marcol's field goal attempt from the Chicago 35 yard line was blocked directly back to him off the helmet of Chicago's Alan Page. Marcol caught the ball and raced around left end, untouched, for the rivalry game's most bizarre ending. The astonished broadcaster Lindsey Nelson called the action with: "Chester Marcol! Chester Marcol! Chester Marcol takes it in!"

* Marcol was released by the Packers on October 8, 1980.

Bears   3 0 3 0 0   6
Packers 0 6 0 0 6   12
Chi   Thomas 42yd FG
GB   Marcol 41yd FG
GB   Marcol 46yd FG
Chi   Thomas 34yd FG
GB   Marcol 25yd return of a blocked FG

12/7
Bears 61-7   **Soldier Field**   **57,176**

Revenge for Chester Marcol's antics in the previous game was sweet. For the Bears. This 54 point win is the rivalry game's biggest blowout and the second worst defeat in Green Bay Packer history.

In the rain, the Bears ran-up 594 yards on the Packers with quarterback Vince Evans throwing for 316 yards and three touchdowns. The game was over by halftime with Chicago leading 28-7. Both Packer quarterbacks, Lynn Dickey and David Whitehurst, threw an interception. Walter Payton resumed his assault on the Packer defense with three touchdowns and 130 yards. Chicago quarterback Mike Phipps was encouraged to throw long and run-up the score well into the fourth quarter.

* At kickoff, it was 56 degrees!

* Chicago's personnel director, Bill Tobin, allegedly decoded the hand signals of Green Bay's offensive coordinator Zeke Bratkowski.

* At midfield after the game, Starr reprimanded Bears' coach Neil Armstrong for Phipps' late passing, the blitzes that were called in the fourth quarter and for putting Walter Payton back in the game with the Bears ahead 55-7.

Packers 0   7   0   0   7
Bears   0 28 13 20   61

Chi Payton 1yd run (Thomas kick)
Chi Payton 3yd run (Thomas kick)
Chi Harper 1yd run (Thomas kick)
GB   Lofton 15yd pass from Dickey (Stenerud kick)
Chi Baschnagel 4yd pass from Vince Evans (Thomas kick)
Chi Earl 9yd pass from Evans (kick blocked)
Chi Watts 53yd pass from Evans (Thomas kick)
Chi Payton 14yd run (Thomas kick)
Chi Walterscheid 36yd interception return (Thomas kick)
Chi McClendon 1yd run (kick failed)

SEASON: Bears 7-9-0 (3rd)   Packers 5-10-1 (5th)

1981

9/6
Packers 16-9   Soldier Field   62,411

The Packers went in front 13-0 and held on. Gerry Ellis and Eddie Lee Ivery paced Green Bay with two first half touchdowns and 166 yards rushing overall.

Chicago's comeback was sparked by Walter Payton and Bob Thomas. Payton scored the touchdown and had over 100 pverall yards for the day. Along the way, Chicago coughed up the ball four times. The most critical miscue came at the goal line with 32 seconds left when Matt Suhey fumbled after being hit hard by Green Bay's Mike McCoy. Johnny Gray recovered for the Packers and Green Bay held on for the victory.

In the third quarter, the Packers' Eddie Lee Ivery injured his same knee for the second time in three years at Soldier Field. He would be out for the another season.

Packers 7 6 0 3   16
Bears   0 0 6 3   9
GB Ivery 2yd run (Wingo pass from Stachowicz)
GB Ellis 5yd run (kick blocked)
Chi Payton 11yd run (Kick failed)
GB Stenerud 33yd FG
Chi Thomas 25yd FG

....

11/15
Packers 21-17   Lambeau Field   55,338

Green Bay sweeps the rivalry game series for the first time since 1972. Quarterback David Whitehurst threw three touchdown passes and the Packers' defense held firm to convert the win.

The game was decided in the first half. With Chicago leading 10-7, Mark Murphy's long interception return setup Green Bay's go ahead score. Whitehurst then closed out the first half with his third touchdown pass and the Packers were in control. Despite another fine performance from Walter Payton (105 yards, 1 TD), the Packers prevailed thanks to Mark Lee's second interception of the day at the Packer 23 yard line half way through the final quarter.

Bears   10 0 0 7   17
Packers   7 14 0 0   21
Chi Roveto 36yd FG
GB   Huckleby 1yd pass from Whitehurst (Stenerud kick)
CHI Suhey 1yd run (Roveto kick)
GB   Huckleby 39yd pass from Whitehurst (Stenerud kick)
GB   Middleton 2yd pass from Whitehurst (Stenerud kick)
Chi Payton 2yd (Roveto kick)

SEASON: Bears 6-10-0 (5th)   Packers 8-8-0 (3rd)

1982

A 57 day strike canceled both of the scheduled games between Chicago and Green Bay.

SEASON: Bears 3-6-0 (12th)   Packers 5-3-1 (3rd)

1983

12/4
Packers 31-28   Lambeau Field   51,147

The rivalry game resumes The teams meet for the first time in more than two years, and the renewal featured more than 850 yards in offense! Gerry Ellis had a fantastic afternoon setting up Green Bay's first points with a 71 yard run from scrimmage. Later in the half, he also scored from 12 yards out to give Green Bay a 21-7 lead. Ellis finished the day with 141 yards rushing.

With 5:30 remaining in the game, the Packers looked ready to close it out with a 28-14 victory. Then a second interception by Leslie Frazier helped Chicago cut the lead to seven. With less than two minutes to play, Dennis Mickinnon's dramatic punt return tied the game and silenced the Lambeau Field crowd.

Fortunately for Green Bay, quarterback Lynn Dickey dug deep and fired a 67 yard bomb to James Lofton to set up Jan Stenerud's winning kick with three seconds left. The loss ended the Bears' hopes for the playoffs while it kept the Packers' slim postseason hopes alive.

Green Bay retired Ray Nitschke's #66 at halftime.

After the game, Packer coach Bart Starr apologized to the team for play calling that almost allowed the game to get away.

Bears   7 7 0 14   28
Packers 14 7 0 10   31
GB   Huckleby 9yd run (Stenerud kick)
GB   Coffman 5yd pass from Dickey (Stenerud kick)
Chi Gault 87yd pass from Jim McMahon (Thomas kick)
GB   Ellis 12yd run (Stenerud kick)
Chi Suhey 1yd run (Thomas kick)
GB   Huckleby 10yd run (Stenerud kick)
Chi Suhey 1yd run (Thomas kick)
Chi McKinnon 59yd punt return (Thomas kick)
GB   Stenerud 19yd FG

....

12/18
Bears 23-21   Soldier Field   35,807

In Bart Starr's last game as coach, the Packers had an opportunity to make the playoffs and save their season with a win. The wind chill reached -28 degrees and the 10 turnovers kept the game close.

Jim McMahon threw for two touchdown passes and scored another himself to save the day for Chicago. The lead went back and forth all afternoon and Green Bay's 64 yard drive with three minutes left put the

Packers back in front 21-20. Chicago came right back, and the Packers offered little reisistance. The Bears marched down the field, and BobThomas delivered the winner from 22 yards out with 10 seconds left. The Bears returned the favor of two weeks ago and eliminatedmthe Packers from the playoffs.

After the game, Starr was questioned for not using his timeouts during Chicago's final drive. He was also heavily criticized for defense's poor performance all year. He was fired the following day.

There were nearly 30,000 no shows.

Packers 7 7 0 7 21
Bears 7 0 7 9 23
Chi Gault 35yd pass from Jim McMahon (Thomas kick)
GB Dickey 1yd run (Stenerud kick)
GB Lofton 31yd pass from Dickey (Stenerud kick)
Chi McKinnon 22yd pass from McMahon (Thomas kick)
Chi McMahon 6yd run (Run failed)
GB Coffman 5yd pass from Dickey (Stenerud kick)
Chi Thomas 22yd FG

Season: Bears 8-8-0 (2nd)   Packers 8-8-0 (2nd)

1984

9/16
Bears 9-7   **Lambeau Field**   **55,942**

Another former Lombardi Packer, Forrest Gregg, became the ninth coach in Green Bay history. Gregg's four-year reign was filled with controversy, particularly against the Bears.

With Mike Ditka now coaching Chicago, it was natural for the two coaches, who were once adversaries on the field, to *up the ante* on the rivalry game. The stakes were raised almost immediately in a *preseason* game in Milwaukee. With benches on the same side of the field, Gregg and Ditka got into a heated shouting match. Players saw first hand the new intensity that would surround the rivalry game as long as these two former players were coaching. In their first official battle, the Packers didn't have enough offense. They ran 45 plays compared to 72 for the Bears. They were held to 32 yards rushing, 10 first downs and 154 total yards. Though the Bears generated 345 yards, it was up to Bob Thomas' toe to overcome Green Bay's lone touchdown.

* There were a number of skirmishes throughout the game. In the first quarter, Charles Martin hit Jim McMahon with what many thought was a cheap shot. Bob Avellini replaced McMahon.

Bears   3 3 0 3   9
Packers 0 7 0 0   7
Chi   Thomas 18yd FG
Chi   Thomas 49yd FG
GB   Clark 1yd run (Garcia kick)
Chi   Thomas 28yd FG

....

12/9
Packers 20-14   Soldier Field   59,374

With 34 seconds to go, Packer quarterback Rich Campbell heaved a 43 yard touchdown pass to Philip Epps to win the game. The pass was underthrown, but Epps came back for the catch. The touchdown was the highlight of Rich Campbell's career. The four year veteran would retire after the season putting an end to a disappointing career as Green Bay's #1 draft choice in 1981. Campbell came into the game in the first half to replace an injured Randy Wright.

The dramatic win briefly overshadowed the phenomenal performance of Walter Payton. Payton ran for 175 yards, scored a touchdown and also threw for one!   But five turnovers ultimately did-in the Bears and damaged their hopes to host a home playoff game.

* This is Forrest Gregg's only win against the Bears as coach of the Packers.

Packers 0 7 6 7   20
Bears   0 0 7 7   14

GB West 3yd pass from Campbell (Del Greco kick)
Chi Suhey 2yd pass from Payton (Bob Thomas kick)
GB Rodgers 97yd kickoff return (kick failed)
Chi Payton 7yd run (Thomas kick)
GB Epps 43yd pass from Campbell (Del Greco kick)

SEASON: Bears 10-6-0 (1st)   Packers 8-8-0 (2nd)

1985

10/21
Bears 23-7   **Soldier Field**   **65,095**

A Monday Night Football game showcased for the nation one of the most infamous moments of the rivalry. Unfortunately, for the Packers, the moment was not very flattering.

Trailing 7-0 in the second quarter, Chicago had the ball at the Green Bay two yard line. Mike Ditka put in the 325 pound, rookie defensive tackle William "The Refrigerator" Perry to block for Walter Payton. After Perry cleared an enormous hole for Payton, touchdown Bears! A short time later, Perry took ran it in himself for six from the one yard line. Before the second quarter was over, the "The Frig" led the way again for Payton. "Sweetness" ran for 112 yards and two touchdowns. But the night belonged to the "The Refrigerator" who became an overnight sensation.

After throwing an interception, Lynn Dickey was hit by Dan Hampton and Richard Dent and forced to leave the game.

There were nine turnovers (Chi 4 GB 5) and several fights.

The unveiling of "The Refrigerator" served notice to the league and the nation about the power of 1985 Chicago Bears!

```
Packers  7   0   0   0    7
Bears    0  21   0   2   23
```
GB Lofton 27yd pass from Dickey (Del Greco kick)
Chi Payton 2yd run (Butler kick)
Chi Perry 1yd run (Butler kick)
Chi Payton 1yd run (Butler kick)
Chi Safety, Otis Wilson sacked Zorn in end zone

11/3
Bears 16-10 **Lambeau Field** 56,895

Lots of talk went back and forth between players and fans before this rematch. After being humiliated by the Bears two weeks earlier on national television, the Packers hoped to exact some revenge.

But the Bears brought the *Super Bowl Shuffle* north to Lambeau Field, and they weren't about to be stopped. Six personal fouls gave the game its usual "punch," and the fun got started when Mark Lee and Walter Payton flew over the Packers' bench after a running play. Lee was ejected. Later, Green Bay safety Ken Stills blatantly leveled Matt Suhey well after the whistle.

Before halftime, "Refrigerator" Perry" outfoxed the Packers again. Split out to the left side, Perry came in motion behind McMahon and caught a touchdown pass for a 7-3 Chicago lead. With the Green Bay clinging to a 10-7 lead in the fourth quarter, a safety and a blistering touchdown run by Walter Payton gave the game to the Bears. Payton finished with 192 yards. In one of the nastiest games in the rivalry's history, 15 penalties were called overall for 136 yards.

The week before the game, the Packers put up posters of Perry to motivate players and coaches.

Before the game, horse manure was delivered to the Bears' locker room.

Bears	0	7	0	9	16
Packers	3	0	7	0	10

GB Del Greco 40yd FG
Chi Perry 4yd pass from McMahon (Kevin Butler kick)
GB Clark 55yd pass from Zorn (Del Greco kick)
Chi Safety, Steve McMichael sacked Zorn in the end zone
Chi Payton 27yd run (Butler kick)

SEASON: Bears 15-1-0 (1st)   Packers 8-8-0 (2nd)
*Beat Patriots 46-10
in Super Bowl XX*

1986

9/22
Bears 25-12   **Lambeau Field**   **55,527**

It's Monday Night Football again at Lambeau. This game was a close one, with field goals providing most of the fireworks. Green Bay led after three quarters, but the fourth belonged to Chicago. With Jim McMahon injured, back-up quarterback Mike Tomczak and the Bears trailed 12-10 in the fourth quarter.

Chicago's defense rose up in the final stanza to take the game from Green Bay. After taking the lead 13-12, Dan Hampton blocked an Al DelGreco's attempt for a fifth field goal. Steve McMichael followed with a controversial safety of Packer quarterback Randy Wright, who thought he had escaped McMichael's grasp in the end zone. Three plays after the free kick from the safety, Bears' third-string quarterback Steve Fuller found Keith Ortego in the end zone for the clincher.

* Packer cornerback Tim Lewis suffered a career ending spinal injury after tackling receiver Willie Gault. He left the field in a wheelchair.

Green Bay ran for only 47 yards, and Randy Wright was sacked four times.

Bears   3   7   0   15   25
Packers   3   6   3   0   12
GB   Del Greco 22yd FG
Chi   Butler 34yd FG
Chi   Payton 2yd run (Butler kick)
GB   Del Greco 46yd FG
GB   Del Greco 45yd FG
GB   Del Greco 50yd FG
Chi   Butler 52yd FG
Chi   Safety, Steve McMichael tackled Wright in end zone
Chi   Ortego 42yd pass from Steve Fuller (Butler kick)
Chi   Butler 27yd FG

....

11/23
Bears 12-10   Soldier Field   59,291

The belligerent play of Green Bay defensive end Charles Martin was the story of this game. Martin tarnished the rivalry like never before with his unsportsmanlike play. In the second quarter, after Jim McMahon had thrown an interception on the opposite side of the field, Martin picked up McMahon and slammed him to the artificial turf like a rag doll. McMahon's shoulder was separated, and he was lost for the rest of the season. So were the the Bears' hopes for a second Super Bowl.

Chicago's Dave Duerson recovered a Green Bay fumble by Gary Ellerson with three minutes left on the Packer 34 yard line! Kevin Butler's kick won it a few moments later.

Like bounty hunters, Martin and Ken Stills wore towels with the numbers of Chicago players on them.

Charles Martin received a two game suspension. At the time, it was the longest suspension in NFL history.

* Green Bay's time out before the kick gave the holder, Mike Tomzak, time to build a small tee in the mud to help Butler kick the winner.

Packers 0 0 3 7   10
Bears   2 7 0 3   12
Chi Safety, Dan Hampton tackled Davis in end zone
Chi Gentry recovered a blocked punt in the end zone (Butler kick)
GB   Del Greco 22yd FG
GB   West 46yd pass from Wright (Del Greco kick)
Chi Butler 32yd FG

Season: Bears 14-2-0 (1st)   Packers 4-12-0 (4th)

1987

11/8
Bears 26-24   **Lambeau Field**   **53,320**

The 1987 players strike did not infringe on the rivalry game. When the owners used *replacement players*, the strike lasted 24 days.

The first game in 1987 was a brutal one with a rivalry game high of 23 penalties for 193 yards. Green Bay held onto a 21-13 halftime lead through the third quarter. In the final period, a Walter Payton touchdown and a Kevin Butler field goal put the Bears back in front. After an Al Del Greco field goal with one minute left put the Packers back on top 23-21, two Jim McMahon passes put the Bears in field goal range quickly. As time expired, Kevin Butler, who had already kicked three field goals and missed two others in the game, nailed a 52 yarder to smack down the Packers.

* Green Bay didn't trust former Bears' receiver Johnny Morris. Now a analyst for CBS, Morris had a tough time preparing for Green Bay. He was barred from practices because the Packers thought he would share information with his former team.

* Kevin Butler gave Forrest Gregg the finger as he left the field!

Bears   7   6   0   13   26
Packers   14 7   0   3   24
Chi Anderson 59yd pass from McMahon (Kevin Butler kick)
GB   West 27yd pass from Wright (Del Greco kick)
GB   Fullwood 2yd run (Del Greco kick)
Chi Butler 27yd FG
Chi Butler 29yd FG
GB   Epps 26yd pass from Wright (Del Greco kick)
Chi Payton 1yd run (Butler kick)
Chi Butler 24yd FG
GB   Del Greco 47yd FG
Chi Butler 52yd FG

....

11/29
Bears 23-10   Soldier Field   61,638

This was Walter Payton's last game against Green Bay. It was also Forrest Gregg's final game against the Bears.

Three weeks after Chicago's last second win at Lambeau, the Bears swept the season series for the third straight year in a rainy and windy Soldier Field. After a touchdown by both teams in the first half, the rest of the game was basically a field goal contest. In the third quarter, after Todd Bell blocked a Green Bay field goal attempt from the 50 yard line, the Bears capitalized with Kevin Butler's second three pointer of the afternoon. The Bears were in front to stay. Max Zendejas, Green Bay's kicker, missed two field goals and lost the field goal contest to Kevin Butler!

Packers 7   3   0   0   10
Bears   0 10   3 10   23
GB   Fullwood 1yd run (Zendejas kick)
Chi Anderson 20yd pass from Jim McMahon (Kevin Butler kick)
GB   Zendejas 32yd FG
Chi Butler 21yd FG
Chi Butler 27yd FG
Chi Sanders 7yd run (Butler kick)
Chi Butler 52yd FG

Season: Bears 11-4-0 (1st)   Packers 5-9-1 (3rd)

1988

9/25
Bears 24-6   **Lambeau Field**   **56,492**

In the first game of the Lindy Infante Era, the Bears ran all over the Packers for 242 yards rushing. Green Bay ran for just 34 yards on the ground and the Bears teed-off on Packer quarterback Randy Wright and sacked him five times.

In the first half, the Packers failed to capitalize on three Chicago turnovers. Though they went in front 6-0, the Bears exploded in the last five minutes of the first half to take control. Walter Payton's heir apparent, Neal Anderson, was impressive with two touchdown runs in the quarter and 109 yards rushing overall.

* Late in the game, Ditka and Green Bay linebacker Tim Harris got into a shouting match.

* Lindy Infante called timeout with 56 seconds left. An angry Mike Ditka then called for a long pass on the next play. The coaches left the field without shaking hands.

Bears   0   17   0   7   24
Packers   6   0   0   0   6
GB   Fullwood 2yd run (kick failed)
Chi   Anderson 45yd run (Butler kick)
Chi   Anderson 4yd run (Butler kick)
Chi   Butler 35yd FG
Chi   Sanders 5yd run (Butler kick)

....

11/27
Bears 16-0   **Soldier Field**   **62,026**

This was the third time in the last five games that Green Bay was shutout. Green Bay's offense sputtered, generating 22 yards on the ground, nine first downs and 189 total yards.

Neal Anderson's spectacular 80 yard run for the Bears was the offensive play of the day. At the time, it was the longest run of Anderson's career. Throughout the game, the Bears moved the ball at will, overpowering Green Bay with 372 yards overall. They stepped up defensively and sacked quarterback Don Majkowski four times. They also chased him out of the end zone for a safety and intercepted two of his passes. Not a good day for the "Magic Man" and the Packers.

Chicago clinched a playoff berth, but they lost defensive end Richard Dent (broken ankle) and quarterback Mike Tomczak (separated shoulder).

Packers 0 0 0 0   0
Bears   7 0 7 2   16
Chi Anderson 1yd run (Butler kick)
Chi Anderson 80yd run (Butler kick)
Chi Safety, Majkowski stepped out of end zone

SEASON: Bears 12-4-0 (1st)   Packers 4-12-0 (5th)

1989

11/5
Packers 14-13   Lambeau Field   56,556

This is the famous *Instant Replay Game*. Trailing 13-7 with 32 seconds to go at the Chicago 14 yard line, Don Majkowski rolled to his right, escaped the grasp of Trace Armstrong, and found Sterling Sharpe in the end zone for what appeared to be the winning touchdown. After line judge Jim Quirk ruled that Majkowski went over the line of scrimmage before he threw the ball, the decision was given to the replay official up in the booth - Bill Parkinson. A tense, five minute wait was worth it for Packer fans as the call was reversed by Parkimson.....touchdown Green Bay! Chris Jacke added the extra point and Packer fans were delirious as they would finally beat the Bears!

* The loss ended the Bears' longest winning streak in the rivalry at eight.

* Packer fans surrounded the Bears bus as it was leaving the parking lot. They rocked the bus back and forth before letting it leave!

* Bears' owner, Mike McCaskey, had an asterisk put next to this game in the Chicago Bear Media Guide.

Bears   3   0   10   0   13
Packers 7   0   0   7   14
GB   Didier 24yd pass from Majkowski (Jacke kick)
Chi   Butler 25yd FG
Chi   Butler 37yd FG
Chi   Muster 2yd run (Butler kick)
GB   Sharpe 14yd pass from Majkowski (Jacke kick)

....

12/17
Packers 40-28   **Soldier Field**   **44,781**

In the bitter cold, the Bears turned the ball over five times yet Chris Jacke of the Packers still managed to kick four field goals. Don Majkowski continued his "magic" by completing 21 of 36 passes for an offense that found the going fairly easy (456 total yards). Majkowski threw one touchdown pass and ran for two more. Green Bay halfback Keith Woodside had a career day with 116 yards and his electrifying 68 yard touchdown run set the pace for this satisfying road win for Green Bay.

* This was Green Bay's first winning season since 1978 (excluding 1982).

Packers 14   10   6   10   40
Bears   7   7   14   0   28
GB   Woodside 68yd run (Jacke kick)
Chi   Muster 3yd pass from Harbaugh (Butler kick)
GB   Kemp 27yd pass from Majkowski (Jacke kick)
Chi   Anderson 21yd pass from Harbaugh (Butler kick)
GB   Jacke 19yd FG
GB   Majkowski 17yd run (Jacke kick)
GB   Jacke 44yd FG
Chi   Anderson 49yd pass from Harbaugh (Butler kick)

GB   Jacke 23yd FG
Chi Muster 4yd run (Butler kick)
GB   Majkowski 1yd run (Jacke kick)
GB   Jacke 21yd FG

SEASON: Bears 6-10-0 (4th)   Packers 10-6-0 (2nd)

Rivalry Stars of the 1980s

Walter "Sweetness" Payton   1975-87   HB

One of the greatest players of all-time, Payton was named MVP three times, and he was a nine-time pro bowler. Payton refused to run out of bounds, ever. He ran for over a 1,000 yards ten times in his career. In 1984, he surpassed Jim Brown's record to become, at that time, the NFL's all-time leading rusher (16,726 yards). Against Green Bay, Payton was outstanding (see Appendix). After his death in 1999, the league's humanitarian award was named in his honor.

Mike Singletary   1981-92   MLB

Mike Singletary was an All-American at Baylor. He was selected in the second round by the Bears in 1981 and went on to become the intense leader of the Chicago defense. Singletary missed just two games in his career, and he was the NFL's Defensive Player of the Year in 1985 and 1988. He was All-Pro eight times and the heart and soul of the great Chicago Bear defense that won the Super Bowl in 1985.

Jim McMahon   1982-88   QB

The Bears selected the talented and brash quarterback from Brigham Young with the fifth pick of the 1982 draft. He started as a rookie and battled injuries throughout his career. McMahon constantly challenged the status quo and often picked fights with the establishment, especially the NFL Office. In 1985, he led Chicago to a Super Bowl Championship. McMahon was the leader of the Super Bowl Shuffle gang and a lightning rod in Bear-Packer matchups.

Chester Marcol   1972-80   K

Marcol was a national soccer star in Poland before coming to America in 1965. He was the NFL's Rookie of the Year in 1972 and a two-time pro bowl selection. Marcol still shares the Packer record for field goals in a season (33) with Ryan Longwell. Bears' coach Abe Gibron nicknamed Marcol the *Polish Prince* for the clutch kicks he made against the Bears.

Lynn Dickey   1976-85   QB

Lynn Dickey of Kansas State was a prolific passer. He threw for more 23,000 yards for Green Bay and Houston. In 1983, he threw for a Packers' team record 4,458 yards that stood until 2011. In the strike-shortened of 1982 season, he led the Packers back into the playoffs for the first time since 1972. His injuries – a separated shoulder and a broken left leg – eventually took their toll and ended his career.

Don "Majik" Majkowski   1987-92   QB

In 1987, the talented *Magic Man* arrived from Virginia. In 1989, he led Green Bay to its first 10 win season since 1972. He beat the Bears in the famous Instant Replay Game (11/5/89). After one of the most controversial games in the rivalry's history, the Packers just missed the playoffs. In 1990, after a disruptive preseason contract dispute, Majkowski tore his rotator cuff in Game 10, and he was never the same.

The Games
1990-99
Wins
Bears 7   Packers 13
Series: 83-70-6 Bears

The nineties produced more teams, more stadiums and more fans. The owners and players reached a new seven year collective bargaining agreement that gave players unrestricted free agency after four years. This was in exchange for a salary cap that protected the owners. Average salaries jumped from $356,000 in 1990 to over one million in 2000!

Billion dollar television contracts with several networks put the NFL everywhere, all the time. Three new teams began play in Carolina, Jacksonville and Cleveland while three others relocated: the Los Angeles Rams to St. Louis, the Houston Oilers to Tennessee (Titans) and the Cleveland Browns to Baltimore (Ravens). It would be no surprise then that when the league celebrated its 10,000th game in 1997, it was played by two of the newer franchises – Seattle and Tennessee. NFL Europe even got in on the action for 17 years with NFL Europe.

Early in the decade, two off the field issues surfaced that remained contentious well into the next century. Current players began using performance enhancing drugs to build stronger and faster bodies at roughly the time that former players began coming forward to receive medical attention for the debilitating effects they had suffered from head trauma and concussions. By the end of the decade, new policies and protocols would take shape around both of these issues.

The rivalry game was much more civilized in the nineties. As Green Bay returned to prominence, emotions did simmer just below the surface, especially when the Packers won 10 in a row from 1994-1998.straight. Green Bay made it to two Super Bowls, winning one, while the Bears never reached the big game. For 16 years, Green Bay quarterback Brett Favre dominated the rivalry like no other player in history (See Appendix). As the new century dawned, the rivalry game remained a top priority and an important measuring stick for both teams. The sign below from the Bears locker room said it best.

"*Redeem Yourself. Beat Green Bay.*"

1990
9/16
Bears 31-13   Lambeau Field   58,938

After the 1989 turnaround, Don Majkowski angered Packer fans when he held out for 45 days before signing a new contract four days before the start of the season. He played for the first time in this game, but by the time he got on the field, the game was over. Anthony Dilweg started in "Majik's" place.

But it was Bears quarterback Jim Harbaugh who stole the show. He threw for two scores and ran for one too. Three Green Bay fumbles led to three Chicago touchdowns, including one fumble recovery by the "Refrigerator." Green Bay turned the ball over five times and the dominant Bears' defense also sacked backup quarterback Anthony Dilweg six times.

* Due to illness, Packer running back Brent Fullwood refused to play in the second half. When he was seen socializing after the game, he was released by Green Bay.

Bears   0   17   7   7   31
Packers 7   3   3   0   13
GB Woodside 10yd run (Jacke kick)
Chi Butler 41yd FG
Chi Anderson 1yd run (Butler kick)

Chi Harbaugh 2yd run (Butler kick)
GB   Jacke 37yd FG
Chi Morris 40yd pass from Harbaugh (Butler kick)
GB   Jacke 37yd FG
Chi Anderson 16yd pass from Harbaugh (Butler kick)

....

10/7
Bears 27-13   Soldier Field   59,929

A steady drizzle and 20 mph winds didn't stop Neal Anderson, who ran for 141 yards and a touchdown. The Packers never got going offensively managing only 32 yards on the ground and 10 first downs. Green Bay quarterback Don Majkowski was ineffective with two interceptions, and, at one point, 12 straight incompletions.

In the first quarter, Chicago tried "Refrigerator" Perry again at the goal line. This time Green Bay stopped him, but on the next play, Neal Anderson scored to put the Bears in front to stay. Though Chicago lost their starting quarterback, Jim Harbaugh, to an injury, they hammered away with nearly five yards a carry and swept the season series.

A plane flew above Soldier Field poking fun at Packer coach Lindy Infante. The sign read: "Lindy's a Girl's Name!"

Packers 3 3 0 7   13
Bears   7 3 7 10 27
GB   Jacke 38yd FG
Chi Anderson 3yd run (Butler kick)
GB   Jacke 27yd FG
Chi Butler 50yd FG
Chi Tomczak 6yd run (Butler kick)
GB   Sharpe 76yd pass from Majkowski (Jacke kick)
Chi Butler 51yd FG
Chi Boso 2yd pass from Tomczak (Butler kick)

SEASON: Bears 11-5-0 (1st)   Packers 6-10-0 (4th)

1991

10/1
Bears 10-0   **Lambeau Field**   58,435

Chicago's defense dominated again and they held Green Bay to five first downs and 141 total yards. The closest Green Bay got to scoring was the Bears' 43 yard line! Jim Harbaugh's short touchdown pass in the second quarter gave the Bears all the points they needed. Frustrated Packer fans booed quarterback Don Majkowski for his poor performance (3-16-32-0-0), and they also let his replacement have it, former Bear Mike Tomczak. Green Bay managed just 68 yards passing.

* Fans were disruptive in the stands and in parking lot. Several citations were issued, and arrests were made.

Bears   0   7   0   3   10
Packers   0   0   0   0   0
Chi   Thornton 8yd pass from Jim Harbaugh (Butler kick)
Chi   Butler 22yd FG

....

12/8
Bears 27-13   **Soldier Field**   62,353

Coach Mike Dikta's 100th win couldn't have been sweeter or any more timely. Chicago pounded the 3-11 Packers to put the breaks on their own losing streak. Brad Muster ran for two touchdowns and quarterback Jim Harbaugh threw for two more to lead a balanced attack.

This time the Packers couldn't run the ball and they managed just 62 yards on the ground. Green Bay quarterback Mike Tomczak turned the ball over twice, once on a fumble and once through the air. The Green Bay defense could not stop Chicago.

* Fifteen penalties were called for 150 yards.

```
Packers   3  10  0  0  13
Bears     7  14  6  0  27
```
Chi   Muster 8yd run (Kevin Butler kick)
GB   Jacke 25yd FG
GB   Harris 1yd pass from Tomczak (Jacke kick)
Chi   Muster 6yd run (Butler kick)
Chi   Davis, 20yd pass from Jim Harbaugh (Butler kick)
GB   Jacke 25yd FG
Chi   Davis 35yd pass from Harbaugh (kick failed)

SEASON: Bears 11-5-0 (2nd)   Packers 4-12-0 (4th)

1992

10/25
Bears 30-10   **Lambeau Field**   59,435

Two new faces shined on the rivalry game for the first time - Brett Favre and Mike Holmgren. The Bears greeted both with a trick play that grabbed the early lead.

As Chris Gardocki of the Bears prepared to punt, a player ran onto the field at the last minute. He was waved off the field because the Bears allegedly had enough players. They didn't! As the player, Mark Green, headed off the field, the ball was snapped. He turned upfield and caught a pass from Gardocki for a huge gain. Brad Muster then took it in from the one yard line and the Bears were off and running.

Kevin Butler kicked three and Jim Harbaugh tied a Bears record with 13 consecutive completions. The streak included a touchdown pass that stretched Chicago's lead to 17-3. Green Bay ran for only 60 yards and were completely dependent upon Favre (20-37-214-1-1).

```
Bears     3  17  3  7  30
Packers   0  10  0  0  10
```
Chi   Butler 18yd FG
GB   Jacke 51yd FG

Chi Muster 1yd run (Butler kick)
Chi Jennings 4yd pass from Harbaugh (Butler kick)
GB   Sharpe 10yd pass from Favre (Jacke kick)
Chi Butler 30yd FG
Chi Butler 21yd FG
Chi Lewis 30yd run (Butler kick)

....

11/22
Packers 17-3   **Soldier Field**   **56,170**

This was Mike Ditka's last game against the Packers. He would be fired at the end of the season.

A steady rain soaked everyone, and 10,000 fans stayed home. The Bears surely wished that Brett Favre had stayed home because he had the first of many outstanding games against them. Favre threw for one touchdown and ran for his first rushing touchdown of his career in the fourth quarter. Edgar Bennett blew through the Bears' defense for 107 yards, becoming the first Packer in 14 games to gain more than 100 yards on the ground.

Packers 10 0 0 7 17
Bears   3 0 0 0 3
Chi Butler 36yd FG
GB   Jacke 39yd FG
GB   Sharpe 49yd pass from Favre (Jacke kick)
GB   Favre 5yd run (Jacke kick)

SEASON: Bears 5-11-0 (4th)   Packers 9-7-0 (2nd)

1993

10/31
Packers 17-3   Lambeau Field   58,945

Halloween in Green Bay was a nightmare for the Bears. Relentless pressure on Jim Harbaugh from Reggie White and the Packer defense produced seven sacks and three turnovers.

Chris Jacke and Sterling Sharpe put Green Bay in front early. A tight game broke Green Bay's way late in the fourth quarter as Bears' quarterback Jim Harbaugh led them toward a tying touchdown. With Chicago on the Packer 12 yard line, a blitzing LeRoy Butler hit Harbaugh as he began to throw. The ball came loose, and Butler recovered it, killing the Bears bid to tie the game. A short time later, Brett Favre led a 91 yard touchdown drive with under two minutes left for the win.

* 60,000 Halloween masks of Packer coach Mike Holmgren were given to fans!

* Reggie White's two sacks of Jim Harbaugh broke Lawrence Taylor's sack record of 132.5.

* The Bears complained that John Jurkovic of the Packers had something slippery on his uniform. Nothing was found.

Bears   0   3   0   0   3
Packers   3   7   0   7   17
GB   Jacke 40yd FG
GB   Sharpe 21yd pass from Favre (Jacke kick)
Chi   Butler, 33-yard field goal GREEN BAY 10-3
GB   Thompson 17yd run (Jacke kick)

12/5
Bears 30-17   **Soldier Field**   **62,236**

Though Chicago's offense didn't score a touchdown, Brett Favre's bad day was all the Bears needed. Favre threw a lot of passes (54) for a lot of yards (402), but he also threw two costly interceptions that were returned for touchdowns. His fumble was also returned for another score. Kevin Butler provided the rest of Chicago's points as they moved into a first place tie with Detroit and Green Bay with four games to go.

* This was the first time in 30 years that the rivals met in the second half of the season with winning records!

* Three defensive touchdowns by the Bears hadn't been done since 1981.

* The Bears would not defeat the Packers again for six years.

Packers 7 0 10 0 17
Bears   7 3 10 10 30
Chi Lincoln 80yd interception return/lateral from Jones (Butler kick)
GB   Sharpe 18yd pass from Favre (Jacke kick)
Chi Butler 29yd FG
Chi D. Jones 32yd fumble return (Butler kick)
GB   Jacke 26yd FG
GB   Clayton 22yd pass from Favre (Jacke kick)
Chi Butler 24yd FG
Chi Butler 29yd FG
Chi Carrier 34 yd interception return (Butler kick)

Season: Bears 7-9-0 (4th)   Packers 9-7-0 (3rd)

1994

10/31
Packers 33-6   **Soldier Field**   **47,381**

This is the first of 10 straight Packer wins, a rivalry game record! It didn't start out that way though as the miserable weather and five consecutive punts weren't encouraging.

A Halloween monsoon on the shores of Lake Michigan complicated matters on Monday Night. The storm brought 30-40 mph winds and horizontal sleet / rain to the stadium by the lake. It dropped 30 degree temperatures into the single digits limiting Brett Favre to 15 passes. Instead, Favre slid to a career high 58 yards, including a 36 yard touchdown run around right end, the longest of his career!

Fullback Edgar Bennett was also impressive. He scored three touchdowns and ran for 105 yards. He scored twice on the ground and caught a touchdown pass from Favre. The Packers' ground game pounded out 223 yards while the Bears picked up just 12 first downs, 94 yards rushing and they turned it over five times.

Over two inches of rain fell and early 20, 000 fans stayed home. The Packers went through two sets of uniforms and over 800 towels!

In the windy downpour at halftime, the Bears retired the jerseys of Gale Sayers (#40) and Dick Butkus (#51).

Reluctantly, former Chicago Bears great, Steve McMichael, played for Green Bay in this game.

Both teams wore throwback uniforms for this game. Green Bay lineman Guy McIntyre commented, "With the uniforms, the weather, the whole ambience of the game was old fashioned"[13]

Packers 0   14   7   12   33
Bears   0   0   0   6   6
GB Bennett 3yd run (Jacke kick)
GB Favre 36yd run (Jacke kick)
GB Bennett 1yd run (Jacke kick)
GB Bennett 13yd pass from Favre (run failed)
Chi Graham 5yd pass from Walsh (pass failed)
GB Cobb 9yd run (kick failed)

....

12/11
Packers 40-3   Lambeau Field   57,927

In the coldest game between them since 1976 (-6 degrees wind chill), the Bears scored first but it was all they could muster as they were blown out again by Green Bay. Brett Favre threw two touchdowns in the first half (three in the game) and the Bears were outgained 517-176. Chris Jacke also kicked four field goals, and the Packers' playoff hopes remained alive.

Bears   3   0   0   0   3
Packers 7   17 10 6   40
Chi Butler 25yd FG
GB Brooks 12yd pass from Favre (Jacke kick)
GB Jacke 39yd FG
GB Bennett 4yd run (Jacke kick)
GB Sharpe 13yd pass from Favre (Jacke kick)
GB Sharpe 22yd pass from Favre (Jacke kick)
GB Jacke 24yd FG
GB Jacke 20yd FG
GB Jacke 29yd FG

Season: Bears 9-7-0 (2nd)   Packers 9-7-0 (2nd)

1995

9/11
Packers 27-24   SoldierField   64,855

Another Monday Night at Soldier Field.......this time, the 150th renewal of the rivalry game!

The first half was all Green Bay while the second half comeback belonged to Chicago. Brett Favre's threw three first half touchdowns including a record 99 yarder to Robert Brooks that gave Green Bay a 21-0 lead. When the Bears held the Packers to a field goal in the second half, Chicago pulled to within three. When Green Bay tried a field goal to extend its 27-24 lead , Ty Detmer fumbled the snap and the Bears recovered. Fortunately for the Packers, Reggie White sacked quarterback Erik Kramer and forced a fumble that was recovered by linebacker Wayne Simmons to end the Chicago threat.

Total Yards: GB 431   Chi 243

In the stands, Ken Ruettgers' wife was pelted with cheese.

Packers 14 10 3 0   27
Bears   0   7 7 10   24
GB   Brooks 5yd pass from Favre (Jacke kick)
GB   Morgan 15yd pass from Favre (Jacke kick)
GB   Brooks 99yd pass from Favre (Jacke kick)
Chi Salaam 1yd run (Butler kick)
GB   Hentrich 32yd FG
GB   Hentrich 39yd FG
Chi Flanigan 2yd pass from Erik Kramer (Butler kick)
Chi Salaam 8yd run (Butler kick)
Chi Butler 20yd FG

11/12
Packers 35-28 **Lambeau Field** **59,996**

The Bears led the Packers by one game when they arrived at frigid Lambeau Field for the second game of '95. They were greeted by a healthy Brett Favre, who was on crutches earlier in the week after a serious left ankle sprain against the Vikings the week before. They also faced Reggie White, who had also been injured in the Minnesota game.

Favre completed his first eight passes which set the tone for an offensive barrage that saw exactly 800 yards of offense between the rivals - Chicago 444 - Green Bay 356. Favre played an extraordinary game (25-33-336) with a career high five touchdown passes. But the Bears struck first when Erik Kramer found Curtis Conway for a touchdown pass in his seventh straight game (Bears' record). Favre then threw two of his five touchdown passes, before Kramer came back to Conway again with seven seconds left in the half to tie it.

After the Bears had gone up 28-21, Favre found Robert Brooks for his fourth touchdown of the day. His fifth came at the end of a 69 yard drive that put Green Bay back in front with three minutes left. The game went down to the end with the Bears running out of time on the Packer 14 yard line.

* Packer fans were ecstatic to see both Favre and White play. They were injured the previous week, and the Bears were very, very suspicious about their quick recovery.

Bears   7 14 7 0   28
Packers 14 7 7 7   35
Chi Conway 21yd pass from Kramer (Kevin Butler kick)
GB   Bennett 17yd pass from Favre (Jacke kick)
GB   Brooks 29yd pass from Favre (Jacke kick)
Chi Salaam 2yd run (Butler kick)
GB   Levens 1yd pass from Favre (Jacke kick)
Chi Conway 46yd pass from Kramer (Butler kick)
Chi Salaam 1yd run (Butler kick)
GB   Brooks 44yd pass from Favre (Jacke kick)
GB   Bennett 16yd pass from Favre (Jacke kick)

Season: Bears 9-7-0 (3rd)   Packers 11-5-0 (1st)

1996

10/6
Packers 37-6   Soldier Field   65,480

A scoreless first quarter quickly turned into a blowout. Brett Favre had his way with the injury depleted Bears tossing three of his four touchdowns (he had a fifth called back) in the first half to put the Packers in front up 20-3. In the third quarter, Don Beebe's 90 yard kickoff return ended any doubt about the outcome.

Green Bay's defense was impressive. They intercepted three Dave Krieg passes. Wayne Simmons' pic in the end zone in the first quarter saved a touchdown and took away any early momentum the Bears had hoped to build. They held the Bears to 53 yards on the ground, and the 31 point victory at Soldier Field matched Green Bay's largest margin of victory in Chicago since 1962.

* Chicago linebacker, Bryan Cox, was suspended and fined $87,500 (one game's pay) for his obscence gestures at the referee after Antonio Freeman's 50 yard touchdown pass.

* Jim McMahon, Favre's backup, played on the last series of downs.

* This was the fifth win in a row for the Packers. It marked the first time since the 1960-1962 seasons that the Packers had won five in a row over Chicago.

Packers 0 20 14 3   37
Bears   0   3   3 0   6
GB Brooks 18yd pass from Favre (Jacke kick)
Chi Jaeger 40yd FG
GB Jackson 2yd pass from Favre (Jacke kick)
GB Freeman 50yd pass from Favre (kick failed)
Chi Jaeger 41FG
GB Beebe 90yd kickoff return (Jacke kick)
GB Freeman 35yd pass from Favre (Jacke kick)
GB Jacke 32yd FG

12/1
Packers 28-17   Lambeau Field   59,682

The Bears led 7-0 with a little over a minute left in the first half. Brett Favre then directed a quick drive downfield and hit Keith Jackson with the equalizer with 54 seconds to spare.

In the second half, Favre went on to have another fantastic afternoon (19-27-231-1-0). He found Antonio Freeman 10 times, and he ran one in himself in the fourth quarter. In utter frustration, the Bears blitzed seven to get to Favre, only to be caught too deep when Dorsey Levens scampered over tackle for a 21-10 lead. The win was Green Bay's sixth straight. The last time that happened was in 1928-30!

Bears   0   7   3   7   17
Packers 0   7   7   14 28
Chi Engram 15yd pass from Krieg (Jaeger kick)
GB   Jackson 19yd pass from Favre (Jacke kick)
GB   Howard 75yd punt return (Jacke kick)
Chi Jaeger 34yd FG
GB   Levens 10yd run (Jacke kick)
GB   Favre 1yd run (Jacke kick)
Chi Engram 6yd pass from Krieg (Jaeger kick)

SEASON: Bears 7-9-0 (3rd)   Packers 13-3-0 (1st)
                                  Beat Patriots 35-21
                                  in Super Bowl XXXI

1997

9/1
Packers 38-24   Lambeau Field   60,766

The Super Bowl Champions opened their season at home against their ancient rivals. The Bears were competitive, and statistically it was a fairly even contest. But again, Brett Favre was the difference by completing 15 of 22 passes for 226 yards and two touchdowns.   Green Bay led 31-11 early in the fourth quarter before the Bears struck twice in the final five minutes.

Chicago linebacker Brian Cox was ejected from the game after arguing with the officials and throwing his helmet. He then got into a shouting match with fans that led to him being spat upon as he made his way to the locker room.

Bears   0 11   0 13   24
Packers 3 15   6 14   38
GB   Longwell 38yd FG
Chi Harris 1yd run (Jim Flanigan from Todd Sauerbrun)
GB   Thomason 1yd pass from Favre (Levens from Favre)
Chi Jaeger 42yd FG
GB   Brooks 18yd pass from Favre (Longwell kick)
GB   Longwell 36yd FG
GB   Longwell 29yd FG
GB   Levens 1yd run (Longwell kick)
Chi Proehl 22yd pass from Kramer (Conversion failed)
GB   Wilkins 1yd fumble return (Longwell kick)
Chi Harris 68yd run (Jaeger kick)

....

10/12
Packers 24-23   Soldier Field   62,212

Green Bay's eighth straight win over the Bears dropped them to 0-7 on the season. But Green Bay barely escaped!

Chicago jumped in front 10-0, and they remained within striking distance most of the game. They outgained the defending champions 353 yards to 227. Brett Favre brought the Packers back with three touchdown passes, two to tight end Mark Chmura. Favre was so hot that with two minutes to go, the Bears went for the win and two points rather than chance giving the ball back to Favre. Unfortunately for Chicago, Erik Kramer overthrew Raymont Harris in the end zone.

Packers   0   14   7   3   24
Bears   10   0   7   6   23
Chi Harris 1yd run (Jaeger kick)
Chi Jaeger 41yd FG
GB   Chmura 2yd pass from Favre (Longwell kick)
GB   Levens 1yd pass from Favre (Longwell kick)
Chi Kramer 3yd run (Jaeger kick)
GB   Chmura 12yd pass from Favre (Longwell kick)
GB   Longwell 37yd FG
Chi Penn 22yd pass from Kramer (pass failed)

SEASON: Bears 4-12-0 (5th)   Packers 13-3-0 (1st)
Lost to Broncos 31-24
in Super Bowl XXXII

1998

12/13
Packers 26-20 **Lambeau Field** **59,813**

The rivals never had to wait this long before playing one another for the first time in a season. In a surprising first half, the Bears held Brett Favre without a touchdown pass and they led 13-9 at the break. But two touchdown passes by Favre in the second half brought Green Bay back. Antonio Freeman caught the winner. The Packer defense held the Bears to just 12 first downs and 192 total yards.

Bears   7   6   0   7   20
Packers 3   6   7 10   26
Chi Stenstrom 1yd run (Jeff Jaeger kick)
GB   Longwell 35yd FG
GB   Longwell 43yd FG
GB   Longwell 40yd FG
Chi Harris 13yd interception return (conversion failed)
GB   Chmura 6yd pass from Favre (Longwell kick)
GB   Freeman 13yd pass from Favre (Longwell kick)
GB   Longwell 24yd FG
Chi Milburn 94yd kickoff return (Jaeger kick)

12/27
Packers 16-13   **Soldier Field**   **58,393**

This very satisfying win made it 10 straight for Green Bay, the rivalry game's longest winning streak!

The Bears led 10-7 at halftime. After Favre had found Freeman for six to put Green Bay back in front, the Bears managed another field goal to tie it. Longwell's short kick with five minutes to go broke the tie. With one minute left, the Bears had the ball at the Packer 33 yard line. Green Bay safety LeRoy Butler then sacked quarterback Steve Stenstrom and forced a fumble that he recovered! Game over.

Packers 7 0 6 3   16
Bears   7 3 3 0   13
GB   McKenzie 28yd interception return (Longwell kick)
Chi Allen 14yd pass from S. Stenstrom (Jaeger kick)
Chi Jaeger 29yd FG
GB   Freeman 8yd pass from Favre (kick failed)
Chi Jaeger 21yd FG
GB   Longwell 18yd FG

SEASON: Bears 4-12-0 (5th)   Packers 8-5-0 (2nd)

1999

11/7
Bears 14-13   **Lambeau Field**   **59,867**

This game was dedicated to the great Walter Payton, who had passed away six days earlier at the age of 45. The Bears came north and beat the Packers in a dramatic finish that would have made "Sweetness" proud. It also fittingly put an end to Green Bay's 10 game winning streak.

Despite losing starting quarterback Cade McNown on their second possession of the day, the game came down to the wire. After the

Packers had driven 73 yards in the minutes, Ryan Longwell's 27 yard field goal attempt was blocked by Bryan Robinson. The block preserved a hard fought, emotional victory for the Bears.

Favre broke Ron Jaworski's record of 116 consecutive starts by a quarterback.

Bears   7 0 7 0   14
Packers   3 7 0 3   13
GB Longwell 37yd FG
Chi Milburn 49 run (Boniol kick) 1
GB Davis 7yd pass from Favre (Longwell kick)
Chi Engram 6yd pass from Miller (Boniol kick)
GB Longwell 26yd FG

....

12/5
Packers 35-19   Soldier Field   66,944

Playing for an injured Dorsey Levens, halfback De'Mond Parker had the game of his life. In cold and rainy Soldier Field, he ran for 113 yards and two touchdowns. His two fantastic touchdown runs in the fourth quarter put the game away. The Bears, who were hoping for two in a row over Brett Favre, kept it close with a third quarter drive and touchdown that cut the Packer lead to 21-19. Favre then orchestrated two fourth quarter drives that were capped off by Parker's touchdown runs.

Packers 0 21 0 14   35
Bears   7   6 6   0   19
Chi Minter 25yd interception return (Boniol kick)
Chi Boniol 24yd FG
GB Schroeder 6yd pass from Favre (Longwell kick)
GB Henderson 2yd run (Longwell kick)
GB McKenzie 45yd fumble return (Longwell kick)
Chi Boniol 23yd FG
Chi Enis 1yd run (conversion failed)
GB Parker 12yd run (Longwell kick)
GB Parker 21yd run (Longwell kick)

SEASON: Bears 6-10-0 (5th)   Packers 8-8-0 (4th)

Rivalry Stars of the 1990s

Kevin Butler   1985-1995   K

The Bears chose Butler in the fourth round out of Georgia in 1985. He remains the Bears' all-time leading scorer (1,116 points), and he made a number of important kicks in the rivalry game. In 1995, Butler was also the last member of the 1985 Super Bowl Champions to be released.

Neal Anderson   1986-93   RB

Anderson was selected by the Bears in the first round in 1986. He was the heir apparent to Walter Payton, who retired in 1987. Anderson played for the Bears for eight years and performed at a very high level. He made All-Pro three times, and he is the third leading rusher in Bears' history.

Jim Harbaugh   1987-93   QB

The Ohio State product was a first round pick of the Bears in 1987. After playing behind Jim McMahon and Mike Tomczak, Harbaugh became the starter in 1990. He was an outspoken leader of the team, and the Bears made it into the playoffs in 1990 and 1991. An injured shoulder kept him out of the 1990 playoffs, and his best season was 1991. Harbaugh is now the coach of the San Francisco Forty-Niners.

☆

Mike Holmgren   1992-98   Coach

Mike Holmgren became the 11th coach in Packer history. He was the quarterback coach and offensive coordinator for the 49ers under Bill Walsh. Holmgren worked with Joe Montana and Steve Young. In Green Bay, he led the Packers back to the playoffs on a consistent basis and took them to two Super Bowls, winning one. Holmgren's record in Green Bay was 75-37 (.669).

Brett Favre   1992-2007   QB

Originally drafted by Atlanta, Favre was the heart and soul of the resurrected Packers. One of the all-time greatest quarterbacks, Favre won three straight MVP Awards in 1995, 1996 and 1997. He played with kid-like enthusiasm, and his gunslinger mentality was exciting and successful far more often than not. He is the NFL's *iron man* with 321 consecutive games played. He won one Super Bowl and set many all-time NFL records including most regular season wins (186) and touchdown passes (508).

Reggie White   1993-98   DE

White helped lead the rebirth of the Packers. One of the most dominant and intimidating defensive ends in NFL history, White shocked the football world when he signed with the Packers in 1993. He brought his tremendous physical prowess to Green Bay, and his impact was undeniable. White became the NFL's sack leader against the Bears (10/31/93), and he made three critical sacks in Super Bowl XXXI. White was an outstanding teammate and a religious leader who was an unstoppable force on the Packers' defense.

The Games

2000-09
Wins
Bears 8   Packers 12
Series: 91-82-6 Bears

Early in the 21st century, both teams opened their newly renovated stadiums. In Chicago, to get fans closer to the field, the seating capacity was reduced from 66,944 to 55,701. In Green Bay, the capacity was increased from 60,890 to 72,515. Pro football's legacy on these hallowed grounds was preserved for the foreseeable future!

The NFL brand continued to have the Midas touch. Sixteen million fans packed stadiums in 2000 and 22 million attended by 2007! When the new Houston franchise began play in 2002, realignment created eight divisions, each with four teams. To cover and promote all the teams, The NFL Network debuted in 2003. Besides the regular season and the playoffs, the league and network had a year round calendar of activities to report on: the college combine, the draft, free agency, off season training activities, mini-camps and training camps! Thursday Night games also started in 2006.

Roger Goodell became the league's eighth commissioner in 2006, and the NFL played its first regular season game in Europe the following year. In 2009, new rules and procedures were put in place for the treatment of head injuries (concussions), including mandatory medical protocol for players before they are allowed to return to the field.

In 2004, the rivalry game got a wake-up call when Lovie Smith became the new coach of the Bears. He proclaimed that his number one goal was to *beat the Packers*. Success came quickly against Green Bay, and the Bears also made their first Super Bowl appearance in more than 20 years in 2006. Green Bay played in the postseason five times in the decade, but they did not reach the Super Bowl. Brett Favre's spectacular Hall of Fame career continued for the Packers until 2008 when he was traded to the New York Jets.

2000

10/1
Bears 27-24   **Lambeau Field**   **59,869**

On the first play from scrimmage, Tony Parrish picked off a Brett Favre pass to set up an early touchdown. The Bears controlled the first half and in the third quarter, Marcus Robinson's second touchdown bomb from Cade McNown pushed Chicago's lead to 24-3.

A ferocious second half comeback by the Packers fell short. Hoping to overcome that first costly pass, Favre brought them back. He threw 48 times for 333 yards and three touchdowns! It wasn't enough as the the Packers couldn't run the ball (44 yards), and they fumbled twice. Paul Edingers' field goal with 3:15 left was the difference.

On the kickoff, Packers' Gary Berry was carried off the field on a stretcher.

Bears   10 7 7 3   27
Packers   0 3 7 14 24
Chi   McNown 1yd run (Paul Edinger kick)
Chi   Edinger 19yd FG
Chi   Robinson 68yd pass from McNown (Edinger kick)
GB   Longwell 42yd FG
Chi   Robinson 58yd pass from McNown (Edinger kick)
GB   Freeman 14yd pass from Favre (Longwell kick)
GB   Schroeder 17yd pass from Favre (Longwell kick)
Chi   Edinger 47yd FG
GB   Schroeder 17yd pass from Favre (Longwell kick)

12/3
Packers 28-6   **Soldier Field**   **66,944**

Sunday night at Soldier Field saw the Packers easily defeat the Bears. Ahman Green scored twice on the ground, and Brett Favre threw for 225 yards and a touchdown. The defense pitched-in with seven sacks of backup quarterback Shane Matthews. They also picked off two passes. Tyrone Williams' fourth quarter interception return for a touchdown put the game away. This was Green Bay's seventh straight win in Chicago.

Packers 0 14 7 7 28
Bears   0   3 0 3   6
GB   Green 2yd run (Longwell kick)
Chi Edinger 32yd FG
GB   Freeman 5yd pass from Favre (Longwell kick)
GB   Green 8yd run (Longwell kick)
GB   Williams 38yd interception return (Longwell kick)
Chi Edinger 46yd FG

SEASON: Bears 5-11-0 (5th)   Packers 9-7-0 (3rd)

2001

11/11
Packers 20-12   **Soldier Field**   **66,944**

The Bears scored the first six points, but after that it was all Green Bay. Chicago couldn't run the ball (47 yards) and their offense produced only field goals. Brett Favre moved the Packers' offense fairly easily, and he connected with Bill Schroeder and Antonio Freeman for two touchdowns. He threw for 268 yards overall, and the Packers moved into first place with the win.

Packers   0 10   7   3   20
Bears   6   3   3   0   12
Chi Edinger 37yd FG
Chi Edinger 47yd FG
GB   Longwell 40yd FG
GB   Schroder 41yd pass from Favre (Longwell kick)
Chi Edinger 38yd FG
GB   Freeman 9yd pass from Favre (Longwell kick)
Chi Edinger 41yd FG
GB   Longwell 31yd FG

....

12/9
Packers 17-7   Lambeau Field   59,869

Brett Favre connected with Antonio Freeman in the first five minutes to give the Packers the lead. The Bears had trouble getting untracked, and they didn't get on the scoreboard until the second half. Overall, they managed just 50 yards rushing and 11 first downs.

The Packers ran for over 200 yards, and they outgained the Bears 352 to 189. Ahman Green's third quarter touchdown broke the 7-7 tie and proved to be the winning points. Green ran for 125 yards in this dominating win.

Favre becomes the first quarterback in NFL history to pass for 3,000 yards in 10 straight seasons.

Bears   0   0   7   0   7
Packers   7   0   7   3   17
GB   Freeman 3yd pass from Favre (Longwell kick)
Chi Thomas 19yd run (Edinger kick)
GB   Green 12yd run (Longwell kick)
GB   Longwell 27yd FG

SEASON: Bears 13-3-0 (1st)   Packers 12-4-0 (2nd)

2002

10/7
Packers 34-21   **Memorial Stadium**   **56,944**

With Soldier Field being renovated, the Bears played home games in 2002 at the University of Illinois in Champaign. The change in location didn't help, as they had trouble running the ball (45 yards), and they gave the ball back to Green Bay four times.

Brett Favre christened Memorial Stadium with three first half touchdown passes. His 85 yard touchdown strike to Donald Driver signaled Favre's continued dominance of the Bears. Ahman Green added 107 yards on the ground, and Kabeer Gbaja-Biamila's 72 yard interception return in the third quarter put the game away.

This is the only Bears' home game in the rivalry series that was played outside Chicago.

Brett Favre surpasses 40,000 yards passing in his career.

Packers 14 10 7 3 34
Bears   7 7 0 7 21
GB Driver 85yd pass from Favre (Longwell kick)
GB Davis 19yd pass from Favre (Longwell kick)
Chi Booker 4yd pass from Miller (Edinger kick)
GB Franks 5yd pass from Favre (Longwell kick)
Chi Davis 1yd pass from Miller (Edinger kick)
GB Longwell 49yd FG
GB Gbaja-Biamila 72-yard interception return (Longwell kick)
GB Longwell 35yd FG
Chi Davis 21yd pass from Miller (Edinger kick)

12/1
Packers 30-20   **Lambeau Field**   **64,196**

In wind chills of seven degrees, two Packers named Walker saved the day for Green Bay. The two unrelated teammates made two great plays that stopped the Bears' bid for an upset.

On the last play of the first half and trailing 14-6, Brett Favre threw a *Hail Mary* pass that was intercepted by Damon Moore. Moore fumbled the ball to Mike Wahl of the Packers who subsequently fumbled to Roosevelt Williams of the Bears. Williams ran nearly the length of the field, and he began celebrating near the 10 yard line. The celebrating allowed Javon Walker of the Packers to tackle Williams and save a touchdown!

In the third quarter, with the Bears on the Packer 10 yard line, defensive tackle Rod Walker snatched the ball away from Olin Kruetz as he snapped the ball. The turnover led to Ryan Longwell's field goal that gave Green Bay the lead. The Packers ran the ball for 181 yards, and Favre threw for 221 yards and two touchdowns.

* *Going into the game, the Packers had lost two straight and Brett Favre was sick.*

* *For the Bears, three different quarterbacks threw the touchdown passes.*

Bears   7   7   0   6   20
Packers   3   3   10 14 30
Chi Lyman 12yd pass from Brad Maynard (Edinger kick)
GB   Longwell 21yd FG
Chi Lyman 8yd pass from Miller (Edinger kick)
GB   Longwell 31yd field goal
GB   Franks 6yd pass from Favre (Longwell kick)
GB   Longwell 27yd FG
GB   Henderson 1yd pass from Favre (Longwell kick)
GB   Fisher 2yd run (Longwell kick)
Chi Robinson 45yd pass from Burris (conversion failed)

SEASON: Bears 4-12-0 (3rd)   Packers 12-4-0 (1st)

2003

9/29
Packers 38-23　　　Soldier Field　　　60,257

A newly renovated Soldier Field didn't bother Brett Favre or Ahman Green. Favre threw three touchdown passes to three different receivers. Green pounded the Bears for 176 yards on the ground and two touchdowns.

The Packers jumped in front fast and never looked back. They roughed up Kordell Stewart with five sacks and intercepted two of his passes. When Chicago narrowed the lead to 24-16 in the fourth quarter, Favre led two touchdown drives to put the game away. This Monday night win improved Favre's record against the Bears to 19-4, including ten straight on the road.

* *Brian Urlacher: "We went out there and laid a big one."*[14]

Packers　17　7　0　14　38
Bears　　0　6　3　14　23
GB　Green 60yd run (Longwell kick)
GB　Longwell 34yd FG
GB　Green 6yd run (Longwell kick)
Chi　Edinger 31yd FG
GB　Henderson 14yd pass from Favre (Longwell kick)
Chi　Edinger 38yd FG
Chi　Edinger, 41-yard field goal
Chi　Thomas 67yd run (Edinger kick)
GB　Walker 9yd pass from Favre (Longwell kick)
GB　Franks 1yd pass from Favre (Longwell kick)
Chi　Stewart 1yd run (Edinger kick)

12/7
Packers 34-21   **Lambeau Field**   **70,458**

Two months later, the Bears got out to an early 14 point lead but lost it with five turnovers. Kordell Stewart was sacked three times and the Chicago's offense couldn't move the ball - 13 first downs, 44 yards rushing. Cornerback Mike McKenzie of Green Bay returned his second interception of the game 90 yards for a touchdown that put the game away early in the fourth quarter. Ryan Longwell also kicked four field goals.

Bears   14 0 0 7   21
Packers   0 13 6 15 34
Chi Booker 61yd pass from Stewart (Paul Edinger kick)
Chi Briggs 45yd interception return (Edinger kick)
GB   Longwell 24yd FG
GB   Longwell 38yd FG
GB   Walker 22yd pass from Favre (Longwell kick)
GB   Longwell 35yd FG
GB   Longwell 45yd FG
GB   McKenzie, 90-yard interception ret (Franks from Favre)
GB   Green 2yd run (Longwell kick)
Chi Azumah 88yd kickoff return (Edinger kick)

SEASON: Bears 7-9-0 (3rd)   Packers 10-6-0 (1st)

2004

9/19
Bears 21-10   **Lambeau Field**   **70,688**

New Chicago Coach Lovie Smith said that *beating the Packers* was his top priority. Success came quickly. In Smith's first game in Green Bay, the Bears snapped the Packers seven game winning streak. Thomas Jones ran for 152 yards, and Mike Brown returned a fumble 95 yards for a touchdown to give the Bears the advantage. The Packers outgained the Bears 404-307, but Brett Favre threw two interceptions and just one touchdown.

Bears   0 14 7 0   21
Packers 3   0 7 0   10
GB   Longwell 25yd FG
Chi B.Johnson 11yd pass from Grossman (Paul Edinger kick)
Chi Brown 95yd fumble return (Edinger kick)
Chi Jones 1-yard run (Edinger kick)
GB   Ferguson 18yd pass from Favre (Longwell kick)

....

1/2
Packers 31-14   Soldier Field   62,197

Since Green Bay had already clinched the division, Brett Favre played only into the second quarter. In his short stint, he still managed to throw for 196 yards and two touchdowns. The defense kept the lid on the Bears' offense by sacking quarterback Chad Hutchinson nine times! The win was Green Bay's 21st in the last 26 games against the Bears and their 11th straight against them on the road.

Packers 7 21 3 0   31
Bears   7   0 7 0   14
Chi Jones 2yd run (Edinger kick)
GB   Franks 17yd pass from Favre (Longwell kick)
GB   Henderson 38yd pass from Favre (Longwell kick)
GB   Sharper 43yd interception return (Longwell kick)
GB   Walker 25yd pass from Nall (Longwell kick)
Chi Jones 1yd run (Edinger kick)
GB   Longwell 20yd FG

SEASON: Bears 5-11-0 (4th)   Packers 10-6-0 (1st)

2005

12/4
Bears 19-7   **Soldier Field**   **62,177**

Brett Favre failed to throw a touchdown pass against the Bears for the first time in 26 games. It wasn't without trying, however as he threw 58 times! Two interceptions turned the tide against Green Bay. The first by, Charles Tillman, was returned 95 yards to set up a field goal. The second, with three minutes left, by all-pro Nathan Vasher, put the game away. Robbie Gould's kicked in 12 points as Chicago's anemic offense generated only 10 first downs and 68 yards passing.

Packers 0 7 0   0   7
Bears   0 9 0 10 19
Chi Gould 21yd FG
GB   Gado 2yd run (Longwell kick)
Chi Gould 40yd FG
Chi Gould 25yd FG
Chi Gould 35yd FG
Chi Vasher 45yd interception return (Gould kick)

....

12/25
Bears 24-17   **Lambeau Field**   **69,757**

For Christmas, Brett Favre threw four interceptions, and the Packers ran for just 65 yards. The Bears won both of the rivalry games for the first time since 1991.

Chicago quarterback Rex Grossman beats the Packers in his first NFL start. With the victory, the Bears clinched the NFC North! Though Grossman threw for just 166 yards, he fooled the Packer secondary often. Then when Lance Briggs intercepted Brett Favre and took it in for six, the Bears led 24-7 at the start of the fourth quarter. Green Bay came back to life a bit in the fourth quarter, but their final drive stalled at the Bears 35 yard line, when Brett Favre was sacked twice.

This was Favre's only losing season in Green Bay.

```
Bears    7  7  10   0   24
Packers  0  7   0  10   17
```
Chi Muhammad 12yd pass from Grossman (Gould kick)
GB Herron 1yd run (Longwell kick)
Chi Jones 2yd run (Gould kick)
Chi Gould 45yd FG
Chi Briggs 10yd interception return (Gould kick)
GB Chatman 85yd punt return (Longwell kick)
GB Longwell 26yd FG

SEASON: Bears 11-5-0 (1st)   Packers 4-12-0 (4th)

2006

9/10
Bears 26-0   **Lambeau Field**   **70,918**

In Mike McCarthy's first game as coach of Green Bay, the Packers are shut out. This was also the first shutout of Brett Favre's career.

Chicago took the lead on their first possession and were never seriously threatened. Robbie Gould's toe kept the score moving after Rex Grossman's bomb to Bernard Berrian. Devin Hester's brilliant punt return put it away. The Bears' defense sacked Favre three times, and Charles Tillman and Danieal Manning each made a second half interception.

This was Devin Hester's first punt return for a touchdown.

```
Bears    7  9  3  7   26
Packers  0  0  0  0    0
```
Chi Berrian 49yd pass from Grossman (Gould kick)
Chi Gould 40yd FG
Chi Gould 39yd FG
Chi Gould 28yd FG
Chi Gould 30yd FG
Chi Hester 84yd punt return (Gould kick)

12/31
Packers 26-7　　　　Soldier Field　　　　62,287

Going into the final game of 2006, the Bears had already clinched the #1 seed in the playoffs and the Packers hoped to finish a strong 8-8. Also hanging over the season finale was Brett Favre's uncertainty about playing another year. This Sunday Night Game was an emotional one for Favre and, he made certain, that if this was his last call, he went out in style. He defeated the Super Bowl bound archenemy on the road one final time!

Favre had a great game (21-42-285-1-1), and he started quickly with a 75 yard touchdown drive on Green Bay's first possession. Rex Grossman passed for 33 yards in the first half, and he threw three interceptions. Two of the picks were returned for touchdowns. Brian Griese replaced Grossman in the second half, but it made no difference. The Bears turned the ball over six times.

* The Bears picked up just 13 first downs and they turned the ball over six times.

** Brett Favre: "If this was the last game, I couldn't be more pleased with the outcome."*15 *It wasn't.*

Packers 13　10　0　3　26
Bears　　 0　 0　7　0　 7
GB　Driver 9yd pass from Favre (Rayner kick)
GB　Collins 55yd interception return (kick failed)
GB　Rayner 25yd FG
GB　Dendy 30yd interception return (Rayner kick)
Chi　Bradley 75yd pass from Griese (Robbie Gould kick)
GB　Rayner 46yd FG

SEASON:　Bears 13-3-0 (1st)　Packers 8-8-0 (2nd)
*Lost to Colts 29-17
in Super Bowl XLI*

2007

10/7
Bears 27-20   **Lambeau Field**   **70,904**

The defending NFC champions, hand the Packers their first loss of the season. In the first half, Bears' cornerback Charles Tillman stripped the ball twice from rookie receiver James Jones. The turnovers killed two promising Green Bay drives inside Bear territory.

With the Packers in front by 10 at halftime, Chicago came back. Brian Urlacker's interception of Brett Favre led to a Chicago touchdown. A fumble by Charles Woodson gave the ball back to the Bears and Robbie Gould tied it. Late in the fourth quarter, quarterback Brian Griese led the Bears on a 79 yard drive that ended with the winning pass to Desmond Clark with two minutes left.

Bears   0   7   10   10   27
Packers 7   10   3   0   20
GB   Wynn 2yd run (Crosby kick)
Chi   Benson 10yd run (Gould kick)
GB   Jennings 41yd pass from Favre (Crosby kick)
GB   Crosby 37yd FG
Chi   Gould 44yd FG
GB   Crosby 37yd FG
Chi   Olsen 19yd pass from Griese
Chi   Gould 36yd FG
Chi   Clark 34yd pass from Griese (Gould kick)

12/23
Bears 35-7   **Soldier Field**   **62,272**

This was Brett Favre's last game against Chicago in a Packer uniform. In 32 games against them, Favre dominated the rivalry game like no other quarterback in Packer history. He won 22 of 32 games. While his career statistics against the Bears are outstanding (See Appendix), in this game he was not.

On a windy and bitterly cold afternoon, Favre completed only 17 of 32 passes for 153 yards. He didn't throw a touchdown pass, but he did throw two interceptions that blew the game open. The first by Alex Brown came on Green Bay's first drive of the third quarter. It gave the Bears a two touchdown lead. The second was the icing on the cake when Brian Urlacher returned a pick 85 yards for six!

The loss ended Green Bay's chances of a # 1 seed in the NFC playoffs.

Packers 0 7 0 0 7
Bears 3 10 15 7 35
Chi Gould 31yd FG
Chi Gould 35yd FG
GB   Grant 66yd run (Crosby kick)
Chi Peterson 8yd run (Gould kick)
Chi Clark 3yd pass from Orton (Orton-Olsen pass)
Chi Graham 7yd return of blocked punt (Gould kick)
Chi Urlacher 85yd interception return (Gould kick) CHICAGO 35-7

SEASON: Bears 7-9-0 (4th)   Packers 13-3-0 (1st)

2008

11/16
Packers 37-3   Lambeau Field   71,040

Aaron Rodgers got off on the right foot in his first rivalry game! The win ended the Bears' two game winning streak over the Packers. It also stopped Green Bay's current two game losing streak.

Rodgers threw for 227 yards and two touchdowns. Ryan Grant led the ground attack with 145 yards. Green Bay's defense did not allow the Bears to get going (holding them to nine first downs) while the Packers' offense was unstoppable, outgaining Chicago 427-234.

The win lifted the 5-5 Packers into a three way tie for first place with the Bears and the Vikings.

Bears   0   3   0   0   3
Packers 7 10   7 13 37
GB Jennings 3yd pass from Rodgers (Crosby kick)
Chi Gould 35yd FG
GB Grant 4yd run (Crosby kick)
GB Crosby 53yd FG
GB Lee 5yd pass from Rodgers (Crosby kick)
GB Crosby 33yd FG
GB Hunter 53yd fumble return (Crosby kick)
GB Crosby 45yd FG

....

12/22
Bears 20-17 (OT)   Soldier Field   62,151

This game was played in -13 degree wind chills. The Packers were almost as cold since they hadn't won since beating the Bears in November.

Green Bay couldn't hold onto their 14-3 halftime lead. Bears' quarterback Kyle Orton brought Chicago back. In a 17-17 game with 18 seconds left, Alex Brown of the Bears blocked Mason Crosby's field goal attempt sending the game into overtime.

In the first possession of the extra period, the Packers couldn't stop Chicago. Orten and Matt Forte drove the Bears deep into Packer territory. Robbie Gould's 38 yard field attempt split the uprights, and the Chicago fans were rewarded for braving the cold.

Packers 0 14   0   3   0 17
Bears   0   3   7   3   20
GB Jennings 7yd pass from Rodgers (Crosby kick)
Chi Gould 31yd FG
GB Grant 17yd pass from Rodgers (Crosby kick)
Chi Olsen 3yd pass from Orton (Gould kick)

GB   Crosby 28yd FG
Chi Forte 3yd run (Gould kick)
Chi Gould 38yd FG

SEASON: Bears 9-7-0 (2nd)   Packers 6-10-0 (3rd)

2009

9/13
Packers 21-15   Lambeau Field   70,920

Chicago's new quarterback Jay Cutler acquired from the Broncos debuts against Green Bay's new 3-4 defense. The new alignment contained Cutler and the Bears well to give Aaron Rodgers a chance to win the game at the end. The Packers were outgained by the Bears 352-226, but they rattled Cutler and picked off four of his passes. With 1:11 left in the game, Rodgers found Greg Jennings for the winning touchdown.

Bears   0   2   10   3   15
Packers   0   10 0   11 21
GB   Crosby 49yd FG
Chi Rodgers sacked by Manning in the end zone
GB   Grant 1yd run (Crosby kick)
Chi Hester 36yd pass from Jay Cutler (Gould kick)
Chi Gould 47yd FG
GB   Crosby 39yd FG
Chi Gould 21yd FG
GB   Jennings 50yd pass from Rodgers (Rodgers to Jennings)

12/13
Packers 21-14   Soldier Field   62,214

Exactly three months later, the Packers swept the season series by a nearly identical score. Ryan Grant ran for 137 yards and two touchdowns in this one. When the Bears pulled ahead 14-13 in the second half, Nick Collins intercepted a Jay Cutler pass and returned it 57 yards to set up Grant's go ahead touchdown. Charles Woodson also had an interception for the Packers. A running game that produced just 59 yards did not allow the Bears to get control the football. Chicago also committed 13 penalties for 109 yards.

Packers   10 3 0 8   21
Bears   0 7 7 0   14
GB   Grant 62yd run (Crosby kick)
GB   Crosby 33yd FG
GB   Crosby 26yd FG
Chi   Knox 19yd pass from Jay Cutler (Gould kick)
Chi   Aromashodu 10yd pass from Cutler (Gould kick)
GB   Grant 1yd run (Rodgers pass to Jennings)

SEASON: Bears 7-9-0 (3rd)   Packers 11-5-0 (2nd)

Rivalry Stars of the 2000s

Brian Urlacher   2000-2012   MLB
The backbone of the Bears' defense during his career, Urlacher was a first round pick out of New Mexico in 2000 and he played at an all-pro level for Chicago for most of his career. With incredible quickness and strength, Urlacher was named AP Rookie of the Year in 2000 and AP Defensive Player of the Year in 2005. He earned four first team All-Pro honors and eight pro bowl selections.

Lance Briggs   2003-   LB
Briggs joined the Bears in 2003 as a third round pick out of Arizona. He teamed with Brian Urlacher to lead the Bears to a Super Bowl in 2006. Briggs was named to the Pro Bowl seven times, and his current contract expires after the 2014.

Devin Hester 2006-2013 KR, R

Hester graduated from Miami in 2006 and he was a second round pick by the Bears. He has been an outstanding kickoff and punt returner. After an eight year career with the Bears, Hester holds the NFL record for the most combined kickoff/punt returns for touchdowns (19) and most punt returns for touchdowns (6).

★

Brett Favre 1992-2007 QB

Against the Bears, Favre wasn't quite as good in the second half of his career as he was in the first half. But he was still very good! From 1992-99, against the Bears, he was 13-3. From 2000-07, he slipped to 9-7. He led the Packers to seven straight wins over the Bears from 2000-03. For his career, he played exceptionally well against the Bears, winning 22 of 32 games and throwing for 53 touchdowns (See Appendix).

Donald Driver 1992-2012 WR

The Packers selected Donald Driver out of Alcorn State in the 7th round in 1999. When he retired in 2012, Driver would hold nearly every important receiving record in Packer history. He was a favorite target of Brett Favre's, catching the pass that broke Dan Marino's in all-time mark of 61,361 career passing yards.

Charles Woodson 2006-2012 CB

Woodson became the Packers' best free agent signing since Reggie White in 1993. After eight years in Oakland, Woodson received one serious offer in free agency, from Green Bay. Many believed his career was on the downturn when he signed with the Packers. Not so. He became the leader of the Packer defense and he was named the AP Defensive Player of the Year in 2009. Thirty eight of his 56 career interceptions have come in the green and gold, and he shares the NFL record with Rod Woodson for defensive touchdowns with 13 (10 with the Packers).

The Games
2010-13
Wins
Bears 2   Packers 7
Series: 93-89-6 Bears

The NFL turned eighty in 2010! One hundred and seven million people watched the opening weekend's games in 2010 on all sorts of channels! The Super Bowl in 2013 was the most watched program in U.S. television history with 112 million viewers. Four million more than last year.! Sadly, though the NFL lost a television pioneer in 2012 when, Steve Sabol, of NFL Films, passed away. Sabol and his father, Ed, told pro football's story in their eloquent weekly shows that reviewed the games, the personalities and hot topics in pro football. They provided the first glimpse inside the NFL and pro football.

Player safety and the health concerns of retirees were front and center in the new decade. New limits were also placed on where defensive players could hit opponents (ie: blows to the head, defenseless hits). Violators received hefty fines and suspensions. New protocols were issued for concussions in 2011, and the NFL established the Player Safety Advisory Panel, chaired by Ronnie Lott and John Madden.

The league's new 10 year collective bargaining agreement also included an additional $1 billion in health benefits for retirees. The $765 million settlement of the concussion lawsuit brought by the retirees received *preliminary* approval from a federal judge in July 2014. The suit concerns impairments stemming from concussions and repeated head trauma: dementia, Alzheimer's, Parkinson's and ALS. Each retiree must decide by October 2014 whether they want to participate in the financial settlement.

The Bears and Packers played the most important game in their history on January 23, 2011. On a frigid night in Soldier Field with wind chills reaching just seven degrees, they played for the NFC Championship! The winner would go to the Super Bowl. In a classic struggle, Green Bay prevailed in the Windy City and went on to win Super Bowl XLV. In the current decade, the Packers have made the postseason every year, and the Bears have made it twice.

2010

9/27
Bears 20-17   Soldier Field   62,179

Penalties, penalties, penalties! A franchise record of 18 penalties for 152 yards set Green Bay back and cost them the game. After they had jumped in front a 10-0, the Bears began a comeback. They cut the lead to three before half, and a scoreless third quarter setup a dramatic final period.

Devin Hester began the busy quarter with a 62 yard punt return to put Chicago in front. After Aaron Rodgers scored for Green Bay to retake the lead, Robbie Gould's toe tied the game and then won it for the Bears. Gould's winner came after James Jones of Green Bay was sandwiched at midfield by Brian Urlacher and Lance Briggs and coughed up the ball. On the Bears' ensuing drive, Nick Collins intercepted Jay Cutler, but a penalty gave the ball right back to Chicago. A critical pass interference penalty then by rookie safety Morgan Burnett put the ball at the Green Bay nine. With four seconds left, Robbie Gould's kick won it.

* *Green Bay outgained Chicago 379 to 276.*

Packers 7 3 0 7   17
Bears   0 7 0 13 20
GB   Jennings 7yd pass from Rodgers (Crosby kick)
GB   Crosby 38yd FG

Chi Olsen 9yd pass from Cutler (Gould kick)
Chi Hester 62yd punt return (Gould kick)
GB   Rodgers 3yd run (Crosby kick)
Chi Gould 25yd FG17
Chi Gould 19yd FG

....

1/2
Packers 10-3   Lambeau Field   70,833

The Packers needed a win to make the playoffs while the Bears, already the #2 seed, hoped to keep them out of the postseason by playing their starters well into the game.

With a 3-3 tie after three quarters, the Bears' had kept Aaron Rodgers in check. Early in the fourth quarter, Rodgers broke through with a short touchdown pass to Donald Lee. He then turned the game over to the Green Bay defense, particularly linebacker Erik Walden, who sacked Jay Culter three times.

With just under five minutes to play, Chicago began their final drive at their two yard line. A playoff berth hung in the balance for Green Bay as Cutler drove the Bears downfield. With time running out at the Green Bay 32 yard line, Cutler tried for the end zone. His pass sailed over Devin Hester's head and into the arms of Nick Collins and the Packers moved on as the #6 seed in the NFC playoffs.

Bears   0   3   0   0   3
Packers   0   0   3   7   10
Chi Gould 30yd FG
GB   Crosby 23yd FG
GB   Lee 1yd pass from Rodgers (Crosby kick)

SEASON: Bears 11-5-0 (1st)   Packers 10-6-0 (2nd)
Beat Steelers 31-25
in Super Bowl XLV

2010 NFC Championship Game

1/23/11
Packers 21-14   **Soldier Field**   **62,377**

After splitting the season series, the Bears and Packers played the most important game in their long history. The NFC Championship Game would determine the conference representative in Super Bowl XLV. The stakes could not have been higher.

Turnovers and injuries decided the outcome. In turnovers, rookie cornerback Sam Shields of Green Bay picked off two passes intended for Johnny Knox. The first one came at the end of the first half to save a touchdown, and the second one ended Chicago's late fourth quarter drive. In the injury department, Jay Cutler's knee injury seriously damaged Chicago's hopes for a second half comeback.

On the opening drive, Aaron Rodgers got things rolling for Green Bay with an 84 yard march and a touchdown. The Packers appeared to take control of the game in the second period when James Starks extended the lead to 14-0. On both drives, Rodgers was perfect.

In the third quarter, with Green Bay on Chicago's six yard line and ready to put the game away, linebacker Brian Urlacher intercepted Aaron Rodgers. Urlacher took off downfield with only Rodgers to beat. Rodgers brought him down just shy of midfield with the most important tackle of his career. It saved a touchdown.

After Jay Cutler had been replaced by Todd Collins just before half, the Packers kept the Bears scoreless through the third quarter. When Collins gave way to Caleb Hanie, the Bears narrowed the lead to 14-7 in the fourth quarter. But B.J. Raji stopped any talk of a comeback when he stepped off the defensive line to steal a pass from Hanie and returned it 18 yards for six! The Bears scored later in the quarter to make it 21-14, but time was running out. Sam Shields put the final nail in the Bears coffin with his second interception of the day. The Packers were going to Super Bowl XLV!

The last time the rivals met in the postseason was in 1941.

There were 15 penalties for 129 yards (Chi 9-89, GB 6-40).

Packers 7 7 0 7   21
Bears   0 0 0 14 14
GB Rodgers 1yd run (Crosby kick)
GB Starks 4yd run (Crosby kick)
Chi Taylor 1yd run (Gould kick)
GB Raji 18yd interception return (Crosby kick)
Chi Bennett 35yd pass from Hanie (Gould kick)

2011

9/25
Packers 27-17   Soldier Field   62,339

In a rematch of the 2010 NFC Championship Game, the Packers got off to a quick start, and never trailed. Aaron Rodgers connected with Jermichael Finley for two first half touchdowns. A third connection with Finely in the fourth quarter put the game away. Rodgers threw for 297 yards, and Ryan Grant ran added another 92 on the ground. The Packers' defense dominated, holding the Bears to just 13 yards rushing.

Packers 7 10 3 7 27
Bears   0 10 0 7 17
GB Finley 6yd pass from Rodgers (Crosby kick)
GB Finley 7-yard pass from Rodgers (Crosby kick)
Chi Sanzenbacher 4yd pass from Cutler (Gould kick)
GB Crosby 37yd FG
Chi Gould 25yd FG
GB Crosby 28yd FG
GB Finley 10yd pass from Rodgers (Crosby kick)
Chi Davis 32yd pass from Cutler (Gould kick)

12/25
Packers 35-21   **Lambeau Field**   **70,574**

A mild Christmas night at Lambeau Field still had plenty of presents for Packer fans. While Chicago outgained Green Bay 441-363, Aaron Rodgers gift wrapped a masterpiece. On the opening drive, he was a perfect 8-8 with a touchdown, and the Packers led 14-3 at halftime.

Green Bay then went on to score on their first three possessions of the second half, and they never looked back. Rodgers threw for 287 yards and five touchdowns. He threw two each to Jordy Nelson and James Jones and Green Bay won its 14th game, the most ever during the regular season.

Bears   0   3   7   11   21
Packers 7   7   14   7   35
GB   Finley 2yd pass from Rodgers (Crosby kick)
Chi Gould 35yd FG
GB   Jones 2yd pass from Rodgers (Crosby kick)
Chi Williams fumble recovery in the end zone (Gould kick)
GB   Nelson 55yd pass from Rodgers (Crosby kick)
GB   Jones 7yd pass from Rodgers (Crosby kick)
GB   Nelson 2yd pass from Rodgers (Crosby kick)
Chi Davis 1yd pass from McCown (McCown run)
Chi Gould 30yd FG

SEASON: Bears 8-8-0 (3rd)   Packers 15-1-0 (1st)

2012

9/13
Packers 23-10   **Lambeau Field**   **70,543**

A Thursday night matchup at Lambeau Field was a disaster for Jay Cutler and the Bears. Green Bay's defense sacked Cutler seven times, and he threw four interceptions. The Bears were held to 11 first downs and 168 total yards!

With under two minutes remaining in the first half, a fake field goal attempt worked when Tim Masthay of the Packers tossed a shovel pass to tight end Tom Crabtree for a touchdown. When Mason Crosby hit his second field goal of the game at the end of the first half, the Packers had all the points they needed.

* Aaron Rodgers was sacked five times.

Bears   0   0   3   7   10
Packers 0 13   0 10   23
GB   Crosby 48yd FG
GB   Crabtree 27yd pass from Masthay (Crosby kick)
GB   Crosby 35yd FG
Chi Gould 45yd FG
GB   Crosby 54yd FG
GB   Driver 26yd pass from Rodgers (Crosby kick)
Chi Davis 21yd pass from Jay Cutler (Gould kick)

....

12/16
Packers 21-13   Soldier Field   62,534

This game belonged to Aaron Rodgers and James Jones. Rodgers threw for 291 yards and three touchdowns. All the touchdowns went to Jones, and the Packers clinched their second straight NFC North title.

Jay Cutler and Brandon Marshall put the Bears in front. The Packers tied it on a 29 yard bomb from Rodgers to Jones. Just before the half, Casey Hayward picked off a Jay Cutler pass at the midfield and returned it to the Chicago 26. Rodgers then found Jones again with 28 seconds left in the first half.

In the second half, the Packers continued to move the ball while their defense kept the Bears in check. For the day, Chicago was held to 12 first downs and 190 total yards. The Packers generated 20 first downs 391 yards.

* Officials called 18 penalties in this game for 195 yards

Packers 0 14 7 0 21
Bears 0 7 3 3 13
Chi Marshall 15yd pass from Cutler (Mare kick)
GB Jones 29yd pass from Rodgers (Crosby kick)
GB Jones 8yd pass from Rodgers (Crosby kick)
GB Jones 6yd pass from Rodgers (Crosby kick)
Chi Mare 34yd FG
Chi Mare 34yd FG

SEASON: Bears 10-6-0 (3rd)   Packers 11-5-0 (1st)

2013

11/4
Bears 27-20   **Lambeau Field**   **78,122**

This long awaited Monday Night match-up featured a devastating injury for the Packers and a huge win for the Bears. It became a game of back up quarterbacks as Chicago's Jay Cutler was ruled out before the game and Aaron Rodgers of the Packers broke his left collarbone when he was sacked by Shea McClellin.

The game belonged to Josh McCown and Seneca Wallace. McCown easily outperformed Wallace, who hadn't played in two years. McCown threw for two touchdowns and almost 300 yards! Green Bay's secondary couldn't stop Brandon Marshall and Alton Jefferies. Along with Matt Forte's 179 total yards, the Bears were a formidable foe.

Seneca Wallace and the Packers couldn't compete. The Bears won at Lambeau Field for the first time since 2007. The win created a three way tie atop the division that would not be settled until the next rivalry game!

Bears   7 10 7 3   27
Packers 10 0 10 0   20
GB   Crosby 30yd FG
Chi Marshall 23yd pass from McCown (Gould kick)
GB   Starks 32yd run (Crosby kick)
Chi Forte 1yd run (Gould kick)
Chi Gould 24yd FG
GB   Lacy 1yd run (Crosby kick)
GB   Crosby 23yd FG
Chi Jeffery 6yd pass from McCown (Gould kick)
Chi Gould 27yd FG

....

12/29/13 > Game #188 > See Page 2

APPENDIX

- ## WINS

1920s	Bears 7	Packers 6 (3 ties)
1930s	Bears 12	Packers 11 (1 tie)
1940s	Bears 16	Packers 4 (1 tie)
1950s	Bears 14	Packers 5 (1 tie)
1960s	Bears 5	Packers 15
1970s	Bears 11	Packers 9
1980s	Bears 11	Packers 7
1990s	Bears 7	Packers 13
2000s	Bears 8	Packers 12
2010s	Bears 2	Packers 7

Bears lead 93-89-6

- ## CHAMPIONSHIPS

Bears (9)
1921, 1932, 1933, 1940, 1941, 1943, 1946, 1963, 1985

Packers (13)
1929, 1930, 1931, 1936, 1939, 1944, 1961, 1962, 1965, 1966, 1967, 1996, 2010

- ## COACHES

Bears

George Halas	1920-29	84-31-17	.744
Ralph Jones	1930-32	24-10-7	.706
George Halas	1933-42	84-22-4	.799
Hunk Anderson ⎤	1942-45	23-11-2	.676
Luke Johnsos ⎦	1942-45	23-11-2	.676
George Halas	1946-55	75-42-2	.641
Paddy Driscoll	1956-57	14-9-1	.609
George Halas	1958-67	75-53-6	.588

Remained Chairman until 1983

Jim Dooley	1968-71	20-36-0	.357
Abe Gibron	1972-74	11-30-0	.268
Jack Pardee	1975-77	20-22-0	.476
Neill Armstrong	1978-81	30-34-0	.469
Mike Ditka	1982-92	106-62-0	.631
Dave Wannstedt	1993-98	40-56-0	.417
Dick Jauron	1999-03	35-45-0	.438
Lovie Smith	2004-12	81-63-0	.563
Marc Trestman	2013 –	8-8-0	.500

Packers

Curly Lambeau	1921-49	209-104-21	.668
Gene Rozani	1950-53	14-31-1	.311
Lisle Blackbourn	1954-57	17-31-0	.354
Scooter McClean	1958	1-10-1	.091
Vince Lombardi	1959-67	89-29-4	.754
Phil Bengtson	1968-70	20-21-1	.488
Dan Devine	1971-74	25-27-4	.481
Bart Starr	1975-83	52-76-3	.408
Forrest Gregg	1984-87	25-37-1	.405
Lindy Infante	1988-91	24-40-0	.375
Mike Holmgren	1992-98	75-37-0	.670
Ray Rhodes	1999	8-8-0	.500
Mike Sherman	2000-05	57-39-0	.594
Mike McCarthy	2006 -	88-49-1	.641

- PAYTON vs. PACKERS 1975-1987

Date	Att	Yds	TDs	Rec.	Yds	
11/9/1975	14	49	1	1	19	
11/30	12	40	1	2	45	
11/14/1976	18	109	1	1	-2	
11/28	27	110				
10/30/1977	23	205	2	1	5	
12/11	32	163	2			
10/8/1978	19	82		5	39	
12/10	18	97	1	3	13	
9/2/1979	36	125		4	49	
12/9	25	115		1	1	
9/7/1980	31	65		4	38	
12/7	22	130	3	1	11	
9/6/1981	19	81	1	4	29	
11/15	22	105	1	2	8	
1982	Strike - No Games					
12/4/1983	16	58		2	13	
12/18	30	148		3	26	0-1 pass., 1 interception
9/16/1984	27	110		3	29	
12/9	35	175	1			2-4 passing, 1 TD
10/21/1985	25	112	2	4	41	
11/3	28	192	1	3	14	
9/22/1986	18	57	1	2	25	
11/23	17	85		1	-2	
11/8/1987	12	49	1	4	21	
11/29	8	22		3	16	
25 games	**534**	**2,484**	**19**	**53**	**438**	

- ## FAVRE vs. BEARS   1992-2007

Date	Comp	Att	Yds	TDs	
10/25/1992	20	37	214	1	
11/22	16	24	209	1	+ 1 rushing td
10/31/1993	15	24	136	1	
12/05	36	54	402	2	
10/31/1994	6	15	82	1	+ 1 rushing td
12/11	19	31	250	3	
09/11/1995	21	37	312	3	
11/12	25	33	336	5	
10/06/1996	18	27	246	4	
12/01	19	27	231	1	+ 1 rushing td
09/01/1997	15	22	226	2	
10/12	19	35	177	3	
12/13/1998	26	42	290	2	
12/27	16	22	153	1	
11/07/1999	27	40	267	1	
12/05	17	24	155	1	
10/01/2000	31	48	333	3	
12/03	19	31	225	1	
11/11/2001	19	32	268	2	
12/09	15	27	207	1	
10/07/2002	22	33	359	3	
12/01	24	42	221	2	
09/29/2003	21	29	179	3	
12/07	22	33	210	1	
09/19/2004	24	42	252	1	
01/02	9	13	196	2	
12/04/2005	31	58	227	0	
12/25	30	51	317	0	
09/10/2006	15	29	170	0	
12/31	21	42	285	1	
10/07/2007	29	40	322	1	
12/23	17	32	153	0	

22 wins   664   1,076   7,610   53
10 losses   (+3 rush tds)

• STADIUMS

Bears
Wrigley Field	1921-1970
Dyche Stadium	1970 (2/27/70)
Soldier Field I	1971-2001
Memorial Stadium	2002
Soldier Field II	2003 -

> **Wrigley Field** *(Cubs Park 1921-26)*
> "The North Wall was about a yard past the end zone. The south end zone was cut short because of the first base dugout. The tarpaulins were placed in certain strategic positions along the sidelines..."[17]

Packers
Hagemeister Park	1921-22
Bellevue Park	1923-24
Old City Stadium	1925-56
Lambeau Field	1957-

(*new* City Stadium - 1957-65)

> **Old City Stadium** *(still behind G.B. East H.S.)*
> "...no locker room for the visiting teams.....in later years, visiting teams would use the basement of East High.....didn't have any restrooms before the mid-1930s..."[18]

Largest Crowds
Soldier Field	66,944	12/5/1999 & 12/3/2000
Lambeau Field	78,122	11/4/2013
Wrigley Field	56,263	12/13/70
Old City Stadium	25,571	9/25/49

Notes

1. Bear Memories: The Chicago-Green Bay Rivalry, B. Gorr, 2005, p. 45
2. Papa Bear: The Life and Legacy of George Halas, J. Davis, 2005, p. 66
3. Packers vs. Bears, G. Swain, 1996, p. 60
4. Mudbaths & Bloodbaths, D'Amato & Christl, 1997, p. 60
5. Packers vs. Bears, G. Swain, 1996, p. 82
6. Mudbaths & Bloodbaths, D'Amato & Christl, 1997, p. 69
7. Closing the Gap, W. Davis, p.107
8. Packers vs. Bears, G. Swain, 1996, p. 218
9. Flesh & Blood, Dick Butkus and Pat Smith, 1997, p. 160
10. www.packerhistory.net (11/3/1968)
11. Packers vs. Bears, G. Swain, 1996, p. 292
12. 75 Seasons: The Complete Story of the NFL, NFL, p. 262
13. Packers vs. Bears, G. Swain, 1996, p. 374
14. Brett Favre: A Packer Fan's Tribute, T. Kertscher, 2008, 127
15. Favre: His Twenty Greatest Games, D. Moe, 2008, p. 223
16. Scrapbook History of Green Bay Packer Football, Zimmerman, 2005, p.17
17. Scrapbook History of Green Bay Packer Football, Zimmerman, 2005, p.18
18. Scrapbook History of Green Bay Packer Football, Zimmerman, 2005, p.18

Books

Bear Memories: The Chicago-Green Bay Rivalry, Gorr, 2005
Brett Favre: A Packer Fan's Tribute, Kertscher, 2008
Closing the Gap, Willie Davis, 2012
Curl Lambeau: The Man Behind the Mystique, Zimmerman, 2003
Favre: His Twenty Greatest Games, Moe, 2008
Flesh & Blood, Butkus & Smith, 1997
Green Bay Packers 2010 Media Guide
Green Bay Packers: A Measure of Greatness, Goska, 2004
Mudbaths & Bloodbaths!, D'Amato & Christl, 1997
Papa Bear: The Life and Legacy of George Halas, Davis, 2005

Packers vs. Bears, Swain, 1996
Scrapbook History of Green Bay Packer Football, Zimmerman, 2005
Vagabond Halfback: The Life and Times of Johnny Blood McNally, Gullickson, 2006

Internet
www.pro-football-reference.com
www.packershistory.net/index
www.static.nfl.com

www.giantcheeseheads.com
www.facebook.com/GiantCheeseheads

Made in the USA
San Bernardino, CA
13 September 2014